# THE RELEVANCE OF THE OLD TESTAMENT FOR THE CHRISTIAN FAITH

## Biblical Theology and Interpretative Methodology

### S.M. Mayo

UNIVERSITY
PRESS OF
AMERICA

Copyright © 1982 by
**University Press of America, Inc.™**
P.O. Box 19101, Washington, D.C. 20036

All rights reserved

Printed in the United States of America

Library of Congress Cataloging in Publication Data

Mayo, S. M.
   The relevance of the Old Testament for the christian faith.

   Bibliography: p.
   Includes index.
   1. Bible. O.T.--Theology.  2. Bible. O.T.--Hermeneutics.  3. Bible. O.T.--Use.  4. Bible. O.T.--Criticism, interpretation, etc.  I. Title.
BS1192.5.M39  1982        221.6        81-40390
ISBN 0-8191-2656-X
ISBN 0-8191-2657-8 (pbk.)

TO     Parmelee
       Stacy
       Kisa

ACKNOWLEDGEMENTS

Permission to use material from the following publications is gratefully acknowledged.

From THE AUTHORITY OF THE OLD TESTAMENT by John Bright. Copyright (c) 1967 by Abingdon Press. Used by permission.

From "Typology--Its Use and Abuse" by Robert C. Dentan. Copyright (c) Oct., 1952 by ANGLICAN THEOLOGICAL REVIEW. Used by permission.

From THE STUDY OF THE BIBLE IN THE MIDDLE AGES by Beryl Smalley. Copyright (c) 1952 by Basil Blackwell, Publisher. Used by permission.

From AN OUTLINE OF OLD TESTAMENT THEOLOGY by Th. C. Vriezen. Copyright (c) 1958 by Charles T. Branford Company, Publishers. Used by permission.

From "The Learned Society in America: Responsibilities and Opportunities" by James N. Settle. Copyright (c) Summer, 1969, by BULLETIN OF THE AMERICAN ACADEMY OF RELIGION. Used by permission.

From THE BIBLE TODAY by C. H. Dodd. Copyright (c) 1946 by Cambridge University Press. Used by permission.

From THE INTERPRETATION OF THE BIBLE by James Wood. Copyright (c) 1958 by Gerald Duckworth and Co., Ltd. Used by permission.

From HISTORY OF INTERPRETATION by Frederick W. Farrar. Copyright (c) 1886 by E. P. Dutton. Used by permission.

From PAUL'S USE OF THE OLD TESTAMENT
by E. Earle Ellis. Copyright (c) 1957
by William B. Eerdmans Publishing Company. Used by permission.

From AN INTRODUCTION TO THE OLD TESTAMENT
by Edward J. Young. Copyright (c) 1956
by William B. Eerdmans Publishing Company. Used by permission.

From THE PATTERN OF RELIGIOUS AUTHORITY
by Bernard Ramm. Copyright (c) 1959 by
William B. Eerdmans Publishing Company.
Used by permission.

From THE SCHOOL OF ST. MATTHEW by Krister
Stendahl. Copyright (c) 1954 by
C. W. K. Gleerup. Used by permission.

From OLD TESTAMENT THEOLOGY, II by
Gerhard von Rad. Copyright (c) 1965
by Harper & Row, Publishers, Inc. Used
by permission.

From THE OLD TESTAMENT AND THEOLOGY by
G. Ernest Wright. Copyright (c) 1969
by Harper & Row, Publishers, Inc. Used
by permission.

From PHILO, FOUNDATIONS OF RELIGIOUS
PHILOSOPHY IN JUDAISM, CHRISTIANITY, AND
ISLAM by Harry Austryn Wolfson. Copyright
(c) 1948 by Harvard University Press.
Used by permission.

From THE WORD OF GOD AND THE WORD OF MAN
by Karl Barth. Copyright (c) 1928 by
Hodder & Stoughton Limited. Reprinted
by permission of Hodder and Stoughton
Limited.

From CONVERSATION WITH THE BIBLE by
Markus Barth. Copyright (c) 1964 by
Markus Barth. Reprinted by permission of
Holt, Rinehart and Winston, Publishers.

From ESSAYS IN BIBLICAL INTERPRETATION by
Henry Smith. Copyright (c) 1921 by
Marshall Jones Company. Reprinted by
permission of The Golden Quill Press and
Marshall Jones Company.

From THE OLD TESTAMENT IN THE WORLD CHURCH
by Godfrey Phillips. Copyright (c) 1942
by Lutterworth Press. Used by permission.

From THE BIBLE IN THE CHURCH by R. M.
Grant. Copyright (c) 1948, 1963 by
Macmillan Publishing Co., Inc. Copyright
renewed. Used by permission.

From NEW THEOLOGY NO. 1 edited by Martin
E. Marty and Dean G. Peerman. Copyright
(c) 1964 Macmillan Publishing Co., Inc.
Used by permission.

From the REVISED STANDARD VERSION OF THE
BIBLE copyrighted 1946, 1952 (c) 1971,
1973 by National Council of the Churches
of Christ in the U. S. A. Used by
permission.

From EXISTENCE AND FAITH: SHORTER
WRITINGS OF RUDOLF BULTMANN by Rudolf
Bultmann. Copyright (c) 1960 by New
American Library, Inc. Used by permission.

From ACCORDING TO THE SCRIPTURES by C. H.
Dodd. Copyright (c) 1952 by James Nisbet
& Co. Ltd. Used by permission.

From "Preface to Hermeneutics" by James
Muilenburg. Copyright (c) March, 1958,
by the Society of Biblical Literature
in JOURNAL OF BIBLICAL LITERATURE. Used
by permission.

From "Biblical Theology and the Rise of Historicism" by Clarence T. Craig. Copyright (c) Dec., 1943, by the Society of Biblical Literature in JOURNAL OF BIBLICAL LITERATURE. Used by permission.

From a review of John Bright's THE AUTHORITY OF THE OLD TESTAMENT by David H. Kelsey. Copyright (c) June, 1967, by the Society of Biblical Literature in JOURNAL OF BIBLICAL LITERATURE. Used by permission.

From a review of Floyd Filson's A NEW TESTAMENT HISTORY by James L. Price. Copyright (c) June, 1966, by the Society of Biblical Literature in JOURNAL OF BIBLICAL LITERATURE. Used by permission.

From "The Problem of Faith and Reason in Biblical Interpretation" by J. Coert Rylaarsdam. Copyright (c) March, 1958, by the Society of Biblical Literature in JOURNAL OF BIBLICAL LITERATURE. Used by permission.

From "The Task of Biblical Theology" by Millar Burrows. Copyright (c) February, 1946, by the Society of Biblical Literature in JOURNAL OF BIBLICAL LITERATURE. Used by permission.

From ALLEGORY AND EVENT by R. P. C. Hanson. Copyright (c) 1959 by SCM Press, Ltd. Used by permission.

From BIBLICAL AUTHORITY FOR TODAY by Alan Richardson and W. Schweitzer. Copyright (c) 1951 by SCM Press, Ltd. Used by permission.

From EARLY ISRAEL IN RECENT HISTORY WRITING by John Bright. Copyright (c) 1956 by SCM Press, Ltd. Used by permission.

From ISRAEL'S SACRED SONGS: A STUDY OF DOMINANT THEMES by Harvey H. Guthrie, Jr. Copyright (c) 1966 by the Seabury Press, Inc. Used by permission of the publisher.

From EXEGETICAL METHOD: A STUDENT HANDBOOK by Otto Kaiser and Werner G. Kümmel. Copyright (c) 1975 by Chr. Kaiser Verlag. Translation copyright (c) 1967 by E. V. N. Goetchius and (c) 1981 by the Seabury Press. Used by permission of The Seabury Press, Inc.

From THE SENSUS PLENIOR OF SACRED SCRIPTURE by Raymond E. Brown. Copyright (c) 1955 by Raymond E. Brown. Used by permission.

From THE LETTER AND THE SPIRIT by R. M. Grant. Copyright (c) 1957 by The Society for Promoting Christian Knowledge. Used by permission.

From MARCION AND HIS INFLUENCE by E. C. Blackman. Copyright (c) 1948 by The Society for Promoting Christian Knowledge. Used by permission.

From "The Problem of Archaizing Ourselves" by G. E. Wright. Copyright (c) October, 1949, by INTERPRETATION, A Journal of Bible and Theology. Used by permission.

From "The Peril of Archaizing Ourselves" by Henry J. Cadbury. Copyright (c) July, 1949, by INTERPRETATION, A Journal of Bible and Theology. Used by permission.

From "Revelation Through History in the Old Testament in Modern Theology" by James Barr. Copyright (c) April, 1963, by INTERPRETATION, A Journal of Bible and Theology. Used by permission.

From "The Interpretation of Scripture: On Method in Biblical Studies: The Old Testament" by David Noel Freedman. Copyright (c) July, 1963, by INTERPRETATION, A Journal of Bible and Theology. Used by permission.

From "On the Interpretative Task" by Eduard Haller. Copyright (c) April, 1967 by INTERPRETATION, A Journal of Bible and Theology. Used by permission.

Reprinted from PERSONAL KNOWLEDGE by Michael
Polanyi by permission of The University of Chicago
Press. Copyright (c) 1958 by The University of
Chicago Press.

Reprinted from "Preface to Hermeneutics" by
J. Coert Rylaarsdam by permission of The University of Chicago Press. Copyright (c) April, 1950,
in JOURNAL OF RELIGION by The University of
Chicago Press.

Reprinted from "Death and Rebirth of Old Testament Theology" by James Smart by permission of The
University of Chicago Press. Copyright (c) 1943
in JOURNAL OF RELIGION, No. 1, by The University
of Chicago Press.

Reprinted from A QUEST FOR REFORMATION IN PREACHING by H. C. Brown, Jr. Copyright (c) 1968 by
Word Books, Publisher. Used by permission.

Adaptation of THE RELEVANCE OF THE OLD TESTAMENT
FOR THE CHRISTIAN FAITH by S. M. Mayo, a doctoral
dissertation submitted to Southwestern Baptist
Theological Seminary. Used by permission.

Adaptation of "Step-by-Step to Bible Study" by
S. M. Mayo. Copyright (c) April, 1976, by The
Sunday School Board of the Southern Baptist Convention in COLLAGE. Used by permission.

From "The Vitality of the Old Testament: Three
Theses" by James Alvin Sanders. Copyright (c)
January, 1966 by UNION SEMINARY QUARTERLY REVIEW.
Used by permission.

From ESSAYS ON TYPOLOGY by G. W. H. Lampe and K. J. Woollcombe. Copyright (c) 1957 by Alec R. Allenson, Inc. Used by permission.

From THE OLD TESTAMENT IN MODERN RESEARCH by Herbert F. Hahn. Copyright (c) 1966 by Fortress Press. Used by permission.

From BIBLICAL PROBLEMS AND BIBLICAL PREACHING by John Reumann. Copyright (c) 1964 by Fortress Press. Used by permission.

From LUTHER AND THE BIBLE by Jan Kooinan. Copyright (c) 1961 by Muhlenberg Press. Used by permission of Fortress Press.

From THE OLD TESTAMENT AND CHRISTIAN FAITH edited by Bernhard W. Anderson. Copyright (c) 1963 by Harper and Row, Publishers, Inc. Used by permission.

From THE OLD TESTAMENT SINCE THE REFORMATION by Emil G. Kraeling. Copyright (c) 1955 by Harper and Row, Publishers, Inc. Used by permission of Lutterworth Press.

From ESSAYS ON OLD TESTAMENT HERMENEUTICS edited by Claus Westermann. Copyright (c) 1963 by John Knox Press. Used by permission.

From ORIGEN by Jean Danielou. Copyright (c) 1955 by Sheed and Ward. Used by permission.

From THE BIBLE IN THE AGE OF SCIENCE by Alan Richardson. Copyright (c) 1961 by Westminster Press. Used by permission.

From THE OLD TESTAMENT IN DIALOGUE WITH MODERN MAN by James Smart. Copyright (c) 1964 by Westminster Press. Used by permission.

From THE INTERPRETATION OF SCRIPTURE by James Smart. Copyright (c) 1961 by Westminster Press. Used by permission.

From NEW TESTAMENT APOLOGETIC by Barnabas Lindars. Copyright (c) 1961 by Westminster Press. Used by permission.

From INTERPRETATION OF SCRIPTURE by A. Berkley Mickelsen. Copyright (c) 1963 by Westminster Press. Used by permission.

From THE OLD TESTAMENT IN CHRISTIAN PREACHING by Lawrence E. Toombs. Copyright (c) 1961 by Westminster Press. Used by permission.

From INTERPRETER'S DICTIONARY OF THE BIBLE. Copyright (c) 1962 by Abingdon Press. Used by permission.

From PROTESTANT BIBLICAL INTERPRETATION by Bernard Ramm. Copyright (c) 1956 by W. A. Wilde Company. Used by permission of Baker Book House.

From "Concerning the Allegorical Interpretation of Scripture," by Paul K. Jewett. Copyright (c) November, 1954, by WESTMINSTER THEOLOGICAL JOURNAL. Used by permission.

TABLE OF CONTENTS

|  | Page |
|---|---|
| PREFACE | |
| Chapter | |
| I. INTRODUCTION: THE PROBLEM OF THE RELEVANCE OF THE OLD TESTAMENT FOR THE CHRISTIAN FAITH | 1 |
|    Statement of the Problem | 1 |
|    Reason for the Problem | 4 |
|    The Importance of the Problem | 5 |
|    The Problem in Relation to Other Theological Studies | 10 |
| II. REPRESENTATIVE ATTEMPTS TO FIND THE RELEVANCE OF THE OLD TESTAMENT FOR THE CHRISTIAN FAITH: PART I | 19 |
|    Interpretation of the Old Testament | 19 |
|    Interpretation of the Old Testament in the New Testament | 21 |
|    Literal Interpretation of the Old Testament | 27 |
|    Allegorical Interpretation of the Old Testament | 37 |
| III. REPRESENTATIVE ATTEMPTS TO FIND THE RELEVANCE OF THE OLD TESTAMENT FOR THE CHRISTIAN FAITH: PART II | 63 |
|    Modern Critical Interpretation | 63 |
|    Current Theological Interpretation | 70 |
|    Typology | 72 |
|    Sensus Plenior | 81 |
|    Existentialism | 87 |

| | | |
|---|---|---|
| IV. | A PROPOSED SOLUTION TO THE PROBLEM OF THE RELEVANCE OF THE OLD TESTAMENT FOR THE CHRISTIAN FAITH . . . . . . . . . . . . | 111 |
| | The Need to Separate Exegesis and Application | 111 |
| | Assumptions Underlying a Solution | 114 |
| | Solutions Proposed by Others | 123 |
| | Clarification of Exegetical Principles | 132 |
| | Principles of Theological Interpretation | 142 |
| V. | IMPLICATIONS OF THE RELEVANCE OF THE OLD TESTAMENT FOR THE CHRISTIAN FAITH . . . . . . . . . . . . | 177 |
| BIBLIOGRAPHY . . . . . . . . . . . . . . . . | | 187 |
| INDEX . . . . . . . . . . . . . . . . . . . | | 198 |

## PREFACE

The nature of biblical theology was and remains a pivotal consideration in many questions about the Bible. The writings of Walter Wink, Peter Stuhlmacher, James Smart, and others, clearly indicate the importance of the nature of biblical theology. Karl Barth's concern of another generation is both an age-old and an ageless question: how does the Sunday sermon relate to modern scientific study of the Bible?

The author contends that the answer to such questions about the Bible is a hermeneutical answer. However, the purpose of this manuscript is not intended to present a hermeneutical methodology per se. The purpose is to show the nature of biblical theology—to show that hermeneutics is a process which includes both the historical and theological, to show that one cannot exist without the other without distorting the whole.

Although the ideas expressed herein were conceived several years ago, they have crystalized in the interim. And, of course, the problems and questions addressed remain virtually the same. Karl Barth's concern for the Sunday sermon has more recent counterparts.

For example, the hermeneutical approach presented herein was presented in a paper which the author read in 1974 at the annual meeting of the Southwestern region of the Society of Biblical Literature. The paper was submitted under the title "Faith and History: Detente." A change in the title was suggested and the paper was subsequently read under the suggested change: "Appropriation of Biblical Scholarship." The suggested change seemed to imply that the pastor or layman who makes use of historical study is not doing biblical scholarship. That is, biblical scholarship only involves the historical study and not application of the Bible.

The changing of the title of a paper to "Appropriation of Biblical Scholarship" has a counterpart in the young pastor, just graduated with an M. Div., who asked the author if it were alright to preach through a book of the Bible. Was it alright to select sermons on successive Sundays from successive passages in the same book of the Bible? In his mind, the study of an entire book of the Bible seemed not able to yield the results necessary for the Sunday sermon.

For the scholarly association, homiletics and methodology for the pastor seemed not to be part of biblical scholarship. For the young pastor, the consistent study of a book of the Bible (historical study) seemed not to be a part of homiletics.

However, homiletics is a part of biblical scholarship. Sermon preparation is biblical scholarship. Also, historical study is biblical scholarship. Certainly, they are not the same thing. Rather, they are parts of one procedural process all of which is necessary. For either to be done without considering the other would be a distortion of the biblical position.

The biblical position is that the biblical writers wrote to encourage faith in the believer or to elicit faith from the person who is not a believer. John 20.31 certainly makes the case very strongly in the New Testament. The writer presented certain information so that the reader might believe. The statement in the Gospel of John can probably be extrapolated to apply to the rest of the New Testament. Likewise, in the Old Testament, the Israelites purposed to pass their faith along to the next generation. The story of the origin of Passover in Exodus 12 makes this viewpoint abundantly clear. The celebration was to be permanent and was to be a means of telling the children the meaning of the celebration.

Biblical theology, then, is the application

of biblical principles to the lives of people living in the present. These principles are best understood when a thorough historical and linguistic analysis of the biblical material has been made. Indeed, faith and history reach not only a detente but a real cooperation in this process.

CHAPTER I

INTRODUCTION: THE PROBLEM OF THE RELEVANCE OF

THE OLD TESTAMENT FOR THE CHRISTIAN FAITH

## Statement of the Problem

The problem of the relevance of the Old Testament for the Christian faith can be stated succinctly but the ramifications are complex. Does the Old Testament have any meaning for the Christian in the twentieth century? Is it a Christian book? The problem has been stated in various ways depending on the viewpoint and emphasis of the writer. One writer, as a result of attending a worship service in England after years of abstention, stated the problem vividly and dramatically.

> Now, returning to it (the worship service) after a long absence, I saw how odd it was that these mild Midland folk, spectacled ironmongers, little dressmakers, clerks, young woman (sic) from stationers' shops, should come every Sunday morning through the quiet streets and assemble here to wallow in wild oriental imagery. They stood up in rows, meek-eyed and pink-cheeked, to sing modestly about the Blood of the Lamb. . . . They sat with bent heads listening to accounts of ancient and terribly savage tribal warfare, of the lust and pride of hook-nosed and raven-bearded chieftains, of sacrifice and butchery on the glaring deserts of the Near East. They chanted in unison their hope of an immortality to be spent in cities built of blazing jewels, with fountains of milk and cascades of honey, where kings played harps while maidens clashed cymbals; one could not help wondering what these people would do if they

really did find themselves billeted forever in this world of the Eastern religious poets. What, in short, had these sober Northern islanders to do with all this Oriental stuff?[1]

Other, less dramatic, statements of the problem have been made. Smart affirms the need to understand the Old Testament and hear its message. He then states, "The basic problem . . . is how a dialogue between God and man that took place and is recorded in the language and thought forms of ancient eras in Palestine can actually be heard, understood, and entered into by modern man."[2]  Clearly, the question of hermeneutics enters into the problem of the relevance of the Old Testament for the Christian faith. If it is relevant, how is the relevance to be determined? J. Coert Bylaarsdam, commenting on the importance of hermeneutics, says,

> Mankind in general can look at the Bible in only one way. Christians (and here I include Jews) can look at the Bible in two ways. In the first place, like all men, Christians can read the Bible as the primary record of the Judeo-Christian religious tradition. The Bible then is the cultural product of a "historic faith"; it is the first installment of the recorded experience of a religious movement with a long history. Its value then is "educational" both for Christians and for others. The Bible is possessed as a cultural object. It introduces us to the past. In the second place, unlike others, Christians can also look at the Bible as the book of revelation. Its value then is not "educational" but authoritative. In this second case Christians do not go to the Bible; it comes to them. It is no longer a record of the past but a present dynamic reality. It is the

medium in which God confronts men as the absolute, demanding decision. It is the book of personal faith that declares man's destiny. It makes us look to the future. It has always been difficult for Christians to reconcile these two ways open to them of looking at the Bible. They have found it difficult to use both at the same time, to make each serve the other, and to combine the result of both in a single constructive whole. They have not known how to relate faith and history. Consequently they have alternated in using the Bible now as the record of a "historic faith" and now as the book of revelation. We are persuaded that it should integrally serve Christians as both at the same time.
. . . . . . . . . . . . . . . . . . . .
How can these two ways in which Christians can read the Bible be used together and organically related in efforts to interpret the Bible constructively for Christian faith? Can biblical and theological scholarship produce a method of interpretation, a biblical hermeneutics, that will serve our age as a ready guide in this respect? The breakdown of now archaic methodologies as well as the present transition in the use of the Bible make the challenge important and pressing.[3]

The problem of the relevance of the Old Testament is included in statements of a larger problem. The Old Testament, as a part of the Bible, partakes of the problem of the relevance of the whole Bible. Expanded further, the problem encompasses the whole concept of the impact of the gospel on the world. Many people feel that the church, and the gospel, has little if any meaning for their lives.[4]

## Reason for the Problem

The reason for the existence of the problem of the relevance of the Old Testament has not been the same in every age. In the experience of Paul with the Judaizing Christians the problem was caused by the clash of the Old Testament legal system with the non-legalistic view of Christianity held by Paul.[5] At Paul's insistence the Jewish Christian congregation admitted that "the external . . . demands of the Old Testament did not apply to the Gentile Christians."[6] In the second century the relationship of the Old Testament to Christianity became a problem for Marcion because he could not reconcile the God of the Old Testament with the God of the New Testament.[7] In the twentieth century this problem has again become acute because of the achievements of historical critical investigation of the Old Testament.

Critical research, by its insistence that any literature is to be interpreted in the light of its historical milieu, has radically pushed the Old Testament far into the past while Christians regard it, in the main, from the viewpoint of its present validity with no consideration for its age. The emphasis of the <u>religionsgeschichtliche Schule</u> on comparative materials showed beyond doubt that Israel and her religion was a part of the milieu of her time.[8] A serious question arises as to how a document which partakes of many elements of its culture--elements which seem so contrary to Christian principles--could possibly be of any value for Christians who have another document which seems to be so much more refined.[9]

In addition, Christians are generally suspicious of a critical approach to the Bible, sometimes with good reason.[10] They therefore resist the results of such efforts. On the other hand, scholars are committed to the critical approach which often must negate the uncritical approach of Christians in the pews.[11] However, there has been a major shift of emphasis from the historical to the theological interpretation of the Bible largely dating from the appearance of Barth's Römerbrief in 1919.[12] The theological emphasis insists that the Old Testament is relevant for the Christian faith. But this emphasis has come from the same kind of scholarship which made it impossible to disregard the ancient qualities of the Old Testament. Such scholarship is not going to give up its earlier achievements. Having pushed the Old Testament into the past, criticism must now devise means by which it can once more be moved forward, without forgetting its historical context, to take its place in the lives of Christians as significant religious guidance.[13] The Old Testament is a book of the past. How can it be interpreted so that it can be a book of the present also? Thus the problem of the relevance of the Old Testament for the Christian faith is a hermeneutical problem.[14]

## The Importance of the Problem

The problem of the relevance of the Old Testament for the Christian faith affects every Christian and every element of Christianity. If the Old Testament is not a Christian book, then it may be ignored by Christians with no adverse effect. It would be of interest only as a book dealing with a religion that is somewhat related to Christianity. Then it would have historical value only and properly be the object of scholarly research but not Christian usage. Such a verdict would probably mean the almost complete obliteration of its knowledge in the minds of the majority of Christians.[15] The Apocrypha has fallen into disuse by Christians in a similar manner.[16]

The importance of retaining the Old Testament and of finding a hermeneutical solution to the problem of its relevance for the Christian faith can be illustrated in several ways. In the first place, the lot of the Old

Testament on mission fields indicates that there
is danger of its being completely rejected in
favor of national literature with resultant aber-
rations of Christianity. Phillips cites the
opinion of a Chinese pastor which reflects the
desire to give up the Old Testament. The Chinese
pastor felt it to be a waste of time to study the
Old Testament and that intending missionaries or
evangelists would do better by studying sociology
or psychology. "Reading the Old Testament is
like eating a large crab; it turns out to be most-
ly shell with very little meat in it."[17] After
an investigation of the use of the Old Testament
among primitive populations in Africa, and peoples
in India and China, Phillips concludes that legal-
ism, whose avoidance was sought by omitting the
Old Testament, and antinomianism have descended
upon the Church. These dangers resulted from
lack of the Old Testament rightly taught.[18]

     A second example of the need for a better
understanding of Old Testament concepts is the
"death-of-God" controversy. The "death-of-God"
controversy, which is a movement in theological
circles as against biblical studies per se, is
representative of attempts to solve the problems
of life philosophically without recourse to the
biblical materials, particularly the Old Testament. It is symptomatic and illustrative of what
may occur when the Old Testament concepts are
neglected or rejected.

     In his inaugural address at Union Theologi-
cal Seminary, New York, James A. Sanders presented
three reasons why the Old Testament will have vitality in the next round of theological debate.
One of these concerns the "death-of-God" movement.
After registering approval of three elements in
the New Theology, namely, intellectual honesty,
affirmation of the world, and iconoclasm, he
moves on to take issue with three basic tenets of
the New Theologians. All three are related to
the doctrine of God. First, while admiring their
honesty, he feels that the New Theologians may

have made their honesty a god. "The biblical God is not subject to the judgments of man's honesty; man's honesty is the subject of God's judgments." To carry Sanders' stricture further one might say that the New Theologians have made a god of themselves. Sanders concludes, "Man's honesty cannot lead to a denial of God. Man's honesty can lead only to a recognition of the limitations of man's honesty." Secondly, he scores their kenotic Christology. "They believe in the Incarnation without a stopper." That is, God has died leaving us with man alone. In order to proclaim the death of God they accept a dualism or radical distinction between the sacred and profane and Sanders' third stricture is directed against this dichotomy between the holy and the secular. The transcendence of God is ridiculed and a god bearing no resemblance to the sovereign God of the Bible is displaced by man. "Only he who fancies man to be god can call his God dead, that is, has convinced himself that there is no truth which transcends man."[19]

These three criticisms plainly indicate that the view of God held by the radical theologians is inadequate. They do not fully or adequately understand and appreciate the doctrine of God in the Old Testament. The importance and value of the Old Testament is therefore obvious. If it is discarded, rejected, or simply ignored, either by theologians or by Christians in the pew, the result will be much the same. The true character of God and of man will be obscured. The proper relationship that ought to exist between God and man will be obliterated. New gods will be erected to take the place of the God of the Old Testament who is no longer known or, at least, not understood. Knowledge and use of the Old Testament is vital to the welfare and vitality of Christianity.

Thirdly, the importance of the problem of the relevance of the Old Testament can be illustrated by citing the experience of two men. Their experience may be indicative of the need for the Old Testament to be relevant in a personal way. One example of personal relevance of the problem is that of Julius Wellhausen, the epitomy of nineteenth-century historical-critical interpretation. In 1882, he withdrew on his own initiative from the theological faculty and became a professor of Semitic languages. His own explanation of his action is quite significant.

> I became a theologian because I was interested in the scientific treatment of the Bible; it has only gradually dawned upon me that a professor of theology likewise has the practical task of preparing students for service in the Evangelical Church, and that I was not fulfilling this practical task, but rather, in spite of all reserve on my part, was incapacitating my hearers for their office.[20]

If Barth's Römerbrief is taken as a beginning point for the new emphasis upon theological interpretation, then Barth himself can be taken as the other example. Barth was taught and trained in the liberal theology of the nineteenth century which was largely subjective and anthropocentric. The rational element was extremely strong.[21]

When Barth finished his university course, he would normally have entered the ministry. But he hesitated because he did not have the personal experience, a concept taken from Hermann, which he felt was necessary. When he did accept a church, in 1909, his problem was not solved. In that year he wrote an article entitled Moderne Theologie und Reichsgottesarbeit in which he discussed the problem.[22] His practice as a pastor did not agree with theory, with the scientific theology which he was studying in order to obtain a doctor's degree.[23] The problem with which Barth wrestled was basically that of faith and reason.[24] Perhaps it would be well to let Barth himself speak of this wrestling and the crisis he felt while in the local pastorate.

> For twelve years I was a minister, as all of you are. I _had_ my theology. It was not really mine, to be sure, but that of my unforgotten teacher Wilhelm Hermann, grafted upon the principles which I had learned, less consciously than unconsciously, in my native home. . . . Once in the ministry, I found myself growing away from these theological habits of thought and being forced back at every point more and more upon the specific minister's problem, the _sermon_. I sought to find my way between the problem of human life on the one hand and the content of the Bible on the other. . . . It . . . came about that the familiar situation of the minister on Saturday at his desk and on Sunday in his pulpit crystallized in my case into a marginal note to all theology, which finally assumed the voluminous form of a complete commentary upon the Epistle to the Romans.[25]

For both Wellhausen and Barth there was a tension between the scientific (historical) and the theological approach to the Old Testament. Each was aware of the need to find relevance in biblical studies. Each came to the conclusion that scientific research alone was insufficient. Each handled the tension in a different way. Wellheusen, yielding to the mainstream of theological currents in his day, chose the historical approach. Barth, yielding to the influence of Anselm,[26] chose the theological approach, although without discarding the scientific or historical approach.[27]

## The Problem in Relation to Other Theological Studies[28]

All areas of theological study are involved in the problem of the relevance of the Old Testament for the Christian faith. At least one writer has called this problem the "master problem of theology."[29] This is but another way of saying that God is one--with one purpose.[30] Therefore, all the pieces of the theological jig-saw puzzle must be joined into a consistent interrelated whole or they become out of joint with each other and with God. However, since the problem of relevance is a hermeneutical problem, it is necessary here only to place hermeneutics in perspective in the theological spectrum.

Krister Stendahl read a paper before a symposium on hermeneutics in 1957 in which he distinguished between biblical studies and theology.[31] He began by voicing a mild criticism of the format of the symposium itself. Held as part of the annual meeting of the Society of Biblical Literature and Exegesis, it was presumably attended largely by biblical specialists. Stendahl wanted some theologians and philosophers present because he believed that the principles of interpretation belong to the discipline of theology rather than to biblical studies per se.[32] The magnitude and the nature of the problem of hermeneutics call for teamwork between biblical studies and theology.[33]

Stendahl made clear the division of interest between the biblical specialist and the theologian, which is indeed a valid distinction. However, he placed hermeneutics entirely within the discipline of theology.

Since the same word, "hermeneutics," may be used in several different ways, it is vital to specify its intended meaning. There are at least two different meanings of this word or two ways in which it is used. With the present theological emphasis in biblical studies, the student of the Bible faces a double task. In the first place, he must determine what the scripture meant historically and, secondly, he must determine what it means for today. Principles or methods of procedure are needed in both instances. A simple designation for these two sets of principles is historical hermeneutics and theological hermeneutics.[34] Considering the nature of the task, the two sets of principles are not necessarily and probably not likely to be the same.

In addition to the above sense in which hermeneutics means theories or principles, the result of using hermeneutical principles can be given another name.[35] The use of the principles of historical hermeneutics produces exegesis. The use of the principles of theological hermeneutics produces exposition or application.[36]

One reason for involvement with hermeneutical issues is the character of the biblical materials. They are ancient documents and must be understood as such. As far as possible the meaning intended by the author in his own historical context and situation must be recovered. However, the era of historicism is no longer in vogue as the sole method of biblical interpretation. The emphasis on biblical theology challenges the scholar to show how his scientific disciplines are relevant.[37] The student of the Old Testament is both spectator and auditor. As spectator the student engages in historical criticism. As auditor, however, "he must appropriate the word himself, the ancient words must somehow become his, he must participate in the live dialogue of the _I_ with the _Thou_."[38] Hermeneutics is, then, a twofold task, historical hermeneutics and theological hermeneutics which issue forth, respectively, in exegesis and application.

[1] Alan Richardson, The Bible in the Age of Science (Philadelphia: Westminster Press, 1961), p. 170, quoting J. B. Priestly, English Journey (1934), pp. 109f.

[2] James D. Smart, The Old Testament in Dialogue with Modern Man (Philadelphia: The Westminster Press, 1964), p. 13. (Hereinafter referred to as Dialogue.) G. Ernest Wright has a similar statement in "The Problem of Archaizing Ourselves," Interpretation, III (October, 1949), 451.

[3] J. Coert Rylaarsdam, "Preface to Hermeneutics," Journal of Religion, XXX (April, 1950), 79-80. The statements of this problem are numerous. Almost every writer in the area of biblical theology and Old Testament interpretation has something to say about it. The whole area of Old Testament theology is related to it. The assumption is made that the Old Testament is vital to the Christian faith and most such theologies are an attempt to understand and interpret it as relevant in its own right. Cf. Walther Eichrodt, Theology of the Old Testament, Vol. I, trans. by J. A. Baker (Philadelphia: The Westminster Press, 1961), pp. 25-35, especially pp. 26-27; Robert C. Dentan, Preface to Old Testament Theology (rev. ed.; New York: Seabury Press, 1963), pp. 96-104. For other statements of the problem, see Bernhard W. Anderson, ed., The Old Testament and Christian Faith (New York: Harper and Row, 1963), pp. 1-7, a problem of hermeneutics. (Hereinafter referred to as OTCF.) Cf. also A. G. Hebert, The Authority of the Old Testament (London: Faber and Faber, Ltd., 1947), p. 8, a problem of the authority of the Old Testament; James Smart, The Interpretation of Scripture (Philadelphia: The Westminster Press, 1961), pp. 65-92, a problem of the unity of the Testaments. (Hereinafter referred to as Interpretation.) Paul Achtemeier and Elizabeth Achtemeier, The Old Testament Roots of Our Faith (New York: Abingdon Press, 1962), pp. 11-16, a popular statement of the problem. A variety of statements of the problem of the relevance of the Old Testament has been

presented in order to show that it can be and has been approached in many different ways.

⁴ Eugene R. Fairweather, "Christianity and the Supernatural," in New Theology No. 1, ed. by Martin E. Marty and Dean G. Peerman (New York: The Macmillan Company, 1964), p. 236. Fairweather attempts to present the two-sidedness of Christian faith without doing violence to either and "makes a strong case for the view that faith and reason. . . . are not in necessary contradiction" (ibid., p. 235).

⁵ Cf. Acts 15.

⁶ Th. C. Vriezen, An Outline of Old Testament Theology, trans. by S. Neuijen (Newton, Mass.: Charles T. Branford Company, 1958), p. 5.

⁷ See below, Chapter II.

⁸ Cf. Krister Stendahl, "Biblical Theology, Contemporary," The Interpreter's Dictionary of the Bible, I, 418-19. (This publication hereinafter referred to as IDB.) The degree to which Israel was a product of her time is an important question in Old Testament studies and one that has not been satisfactorily answered. However, hardly any serious scholar of the Old Testament would object to saying that there is evidence of cultural influence on Israel. See Edward R. Dalglish, Psalm Fifty-one in the Light of Ancient Near Eastern Patternism (Lieden: E. J. Brill, 1962), for an attempted solution of this problem. Cf. H. Frankfort, The Problem of Similarity in Ancient Near Eastern Religions (Oxford: Clarendon Press, 1951).

⁹ The "holy war" is an example of such an "unchristian" element.

¹⁰ The Liberal school of the last century often reduced the Bible to no more than a book among books. That is, it was a religious book

that could be explained solely as a product of human thought and should therefore be treated in the same manner as other ancient religious material. The same tendency is present today. A critical approach tends to ignore or even suppress any transcendent or divine element that may be present. An awareness of this is expressed by G. Ernest Wright when he says that conservative affinities for Albright's work--which has given historical value to much of the Old Testament again--may be a misunderstanding of Albright's basic liberalism (as against fundamentalism). See G. Ernest Wright, "Old Testament Scholarship in Prospect," Journal of Bible and Religion, XXVIII (April, 1960), 182-93, n. 1.

[11] This is not to say necessarily that scholars do not reverence the Bible as a divine book which has transcendent elements.

[12] Cf. R. M. Grant, The Bible in the Church (New York: The Macmillan Company, 1948), pp. 158-75; Stendahl, "Biblical Theology," pp. 418-19.

[13] Smart, Interpretation, p. 38. Smart, Dialogue, pp. 15-17, has characterized these two methods of interpreting the Old Testament as literalist and critical. Hebert, The Authority of the Old Testament, has characterized the problem as one of conscience for the person who comes to the Bible both as a scientific historian and as a Christian believer. Herbert F. Hahn, The Old Testament in Modern Research (expanded ed.; Philadelphia: Fortress Press, 1966), p. xi, believes that the movement toward theological interpretation is a crisis growing out of a "loss of confidence in the historical approach of many who formerly favored it." (Hereinafter referred to as OTMR.)

[14] Cf. Stendahl, "Biblical Theology," p. 422. The fact that Smart titles his prolegomena to

biblical theology *The Interpretation of Scripture* indicates the centrality of hermeneutics.

15 Cf. Smart, *Interpretation*, p. 40.

16 The intention here is not to say that the Apocrypha ranks with the Old Testament as authoritative Scripture, but that it was more familiar to Christians when it was bound integrally with the Old Testament. Cf. Bruce M. Metzger, *An Introduction to the Apocrypha* (New York: Oxford University Press, 1957), p. vii; chapter 17 contains a history of the Apocrypha in the Christian Church.

17 Godfrey E. Phillips, *The Old Testament in the World Church* (London: Lutterworth Press, 1942), p. 23; see also H. H. Rowley, *The Faith of Israel* (London: SCM Press, 1956), p. 13, n. 3.

18 Phillips, *The Old Testament in the World Church*, pp. 95-97.

19 James Alvin Sanders, "The Vitality of the Old Testament: Three Theses," *Union Seminary Quarterly Review*, XXI (January, 1966), 178-80.

20 Cited by Alfred Jepsen, "The Scientific Study of the Old Testament," *Essays on Old Testament Hermeneutics*, ed. by Claus Westermann (Richmond: John Knox Press, 1963), p. 247. (This publication hereinafter referred to as *Essays*.)

21 Peter Halman Monsma, *Karl Barth's Idea of Revelation* (Somerville, N. J.: Somerset Press, Inc., 1937), pp. 15-16.

22 *Ibid.*, p. 32, citing *Zeitschrift für Theologie und Kirche* (1909).

23 *Ibid.*, p. 35.

24 *Ibid.*, pp. 28, 43, 48.

[25] Karl Barth, The Word of God and the Word of Man, trans. by Douglas Horton (London: Hodder and Stoughton, Ltd., 1928), pp. 100-101. The quotation is taken from a lecture delivered in 1922. The early Barth has been cited as an example of the problem of the relevance of the Old Testament for the Christian faith. Macquarrie seems to feel that the early Barth may be more significant than the later Barth. Macquarrie cites E. P. Dickey as apparently right that Barth will probably be better known by his earlier works. John Macquarrie, Twentieth-Century Religious Thought (New York; Harper & Row, Publishers, 1963), p. 321, n. 2.

[26] Karl Barth, Anselm: Fides Quaerens Intellectum, trans. by Ian Robertson (Richmond, Va.: John Knox Press, 1960).

[27] Cf. Richardson, The Bible in the Age of Science, pp. 88-99.

[28] Another title, adequately describing this section, could have been used: "The Place of Hermeneutics in Biblical Studies."

[29] Emil G. Kraeling, The Old Testament Since the Reformation (New York: Harper & Brothers, 1955), p. 8. Cf. G. Ernest Wright, "The Problem of Archaizing Ourselves," p. 452.

[30] Cf. James D. Smart, "The Need for a Biblical Theology," Religion in Life, XXVI (Winter, 1956-57), 27.

[31] The symposium was a part of the annual meeting of the Society of Biblical Literature and Exegesis, December 30, 1957 and reported in Journal of Biblical LIterature, LXXVII (March, 1958), 18.

[32] K. Stendahl, "Implications of Form-Criticism and Tradition-Criticism for Biblical Interpretation," Journal of Biblical Literature,

LXXVII (March, 1958), 33. Cf. a similar statement by Stendahl in "Method in the Study of Biblical Theology," The Bible in Modern Scholarship, ed. by J. Philip Hyatt (Nashville: Abingdon Press, 1965), p. 206.

[33] Stendahl, "Implications of Form-Criticism," p. 33.

[34] "Theological hermeneutics" is synonymous with what Stendahl apparently means by hermeneutics. "Theological hermeneutics" is used synonymously with biblical theology by Amos N. Wilder, "New Testament Hermeneutics Today," Current Issues in New Testament Interpretation, ed. by William Klassen and Graydon F. Snyder (New York: Harper & Row, 1962), p. 39. Smart, Interpretation, p. 37, uses "historical interpretation" to designate what is here called "historical hermeneutics." Hahn distinguishes between historical interpretation and theological emphasis, OTMR, pp. 261-62, xi-xii. John Bright, The Authority of the Old Testament (Nashville: Abingdon Press, 1967), p. 88, uses "theological interpretation" synonymously with application. (Hereinafter referred to as Authority.) The intent here is to identify historical hermeneutics with modern scientific interpretation and theological interpretation with biblical theology (see Chapter III). "Interpretation" and "hermeneutics" are used interchangeably in the present discussion.

[35] On the distinction between principles and activity see K. Grobel, "Interpretation, History and Principles," IDB, II, 718. Cf. Bright, Authroity, p. 92, for a different view of the terminology describing the interpretive process. Bright feels that "hermeneutics" is the entire interpretive process with "exegesis" as the first step in the process.

[36] Smart, Interpretation, p. 21. Smart also states that both exegesis and exposition must

be a part of the work of both the scholar and the preacher. Similarly, Craig affirms that there are no theological interpretations, only interpreters with a theological bent. Clarence T. Craig, "Biblical Theology and the Rise of Historicism," <u>Journal of Biblical Literature</u>, LXII (December, 1943), 291.

[37] J. Coert Rylaarsdam, "The Problem of Faith and History in Biblical Interpretation," <u>Journal of Biblical Literature</u>, LXXVII (March, 1958), 27. Cf. Grobel, "Interpretation," pp. 718-19.

[38] James Muilenburg, "Preface to Hermeneutics," <u>Journal of Biblical Literature</u>. LXXVII (March, 1958), 22.

CHAPTER II

REPRESENTATIVE ATTEMPTS TO FIND THE RELEVANCE OF THE OLD TESTAMENT FOR THE CHRISTIAN FAITH: PART I

Although the twofold quality of the hermeneutical task has received emphasis in the last few decades, its origin is not due primarily to the development of biblical theology in the twentieth century or to the thoroughgoing use of historical hermeneutics in the nineteenth and twentieth centuries. A presentation of some representative methods of interpretation will help to reveal this twofold emphasis throughout the history of Old Testament interpretation.[1] Although it may be anachronistic to label early Christian biblical studies as historical or theological, these two emphases are apparent.

There have been two extremes in the use of the Old Testament.[2] On the one hand, some have discarded it. Such was the course followed by Marcion in the second Christian century,[3] thus illustrating that this problem occurred early in Christian history. On the other hand, the testimony of the Church, generally, has been that the Old Testament is Christian Scripture. The Church has not been willing to give up the Old Testament and is not willing to do so in the twentieth century. But this decision did not and has not solved the problem of the relevance of the Old Testament for the Christian faith. Beginning in the Old Testament itself, the question of how to interpret the Old Testament has been a problem through much, if not all, of the history of the Church. One writer has called church history the history of the interpretation of the Bible.[4]

## Interpretation in the Old Testament[5]

One of the major developments in Old Testament science has been directly related to

the subject of interpretation in the Old Testament.
That is, when men began to study the Old Testament
from a rational point of view[6] they began to discover various levels in the Old Testament. Not all
the books were written at the same time. In fact,
levels, or documents, were discovered within many
individual books. Such is the case with Genesis
and the rest of the Pentateuch. At the heart of
the documentary hypothesis is the foundational
understanding that various documents were written
at different times and later compiled. In many
instances, this compilation also involved interpretation.[7] The presence of two accounts of creation
in Genesis is indicative of this kind of interpretation.[8] In addition, the material in Kings is reinterpreted in Chronicles. The focus of attention
in Chronicles is upon the Southern Kingdom. The
purpose was to show that a pure tradition had been
preserved in Judah, not in Israel, which at the
time of the compilation of Chronicles was occupied
by the Samaritans. The great personalities of
Judah are idealized in Chronicles.[9]

To describe fully interpretation in the Old
Testament would be to write a history of Old Testament criticism and a résumé of the trends and emphases of Old Testament studies today.[10] However,
if students of the Bible knew how Israel interpreted the early documents and the developing parts
of the Old Testament canon and how she found them,
or made them, relevant, they might find a clue as
to how the Old Testament can be used today. Obviously new materials were added to the canon from
time to time and old materials were reinterpreted.
The method by which this was done might serve as a
clue to the way in which the old material--the Old
Testament canon of thirty-nine books--can be used
today as it is related to new materials and a new
milieu. What method of interpretation did Israel
use in relating new material to the old? On what
basis were books accepted or rejected?

Although the methods of interpretation
used in the Old Testament are not fully known,

there is little doubt that real events were interpreted. The Hebrew people were not unaware of their history. Alan Richardson broadly classifies interpretation in the Old Testament as historical. By this he means that when interpretation took place the writers interpreted previous events as real events.[11]

Also Israel had a sense of freedom in the use of the older materials.[12] The older material was not forced to conform in every detail to the new interpretation and it was not distorted by the new interpretation. The new material was simply set alongside the old material so that the essential message of God would be applicable to a new age. Thus it is possible to say that the emphasis which is here described as historical interpretation formed a part of the process. However, the evidence of reinterpretation also indicates that there was a reconstruction of the historical events similar to the present emphasis on theological interpretation whether on the more radical scale advocated by Noth or the less radical scale advocated by Bright.[13]

## Interpretation of the Old Testament in the New Testament[14]

Following the example of a long history in which the developing parts of the Old Testament canon were constantly being reinterpreted, the New Testament writers also reinterpreted the Old Testament to serve their particular needs.[15] The New Testament use or reinterpretation of the Old Testament evidently was not out of character with the traditions of biblical interpretation in Israel.[16]

The New Testament depended upon the Old Testament for many of its concepts and much of its language. Consequently, "the trend of recent years to seek from the OT itself the source and meaning of NT thought has been an entirely proper one."[17] As a consequence, the large dependence of the New Testament upon the Old for both its terms and its ideas is generally recognized by biblical scholarship today. Therefore, we may expect to find evidence of the historical and theological emphases in the New Testament as well as in the Old Testament.

Recent surveys of the use of the Old Testament by the New Testament have begun to inform biblical studies about the interpretative methodology used by the New Testament writers. Primarily, researchers have investigated the use of the Old Testament by Jesus[18] and by Paul.[19] Some studies have been general in nature.[20]

Krister Stendahl's major contribution has been to suggest the existence of a "school" in the early Church which used a method of interpretation that differed from the halakic and haggadic methods favored by the rabbinic schools.[21] The particular method of interpretation employed by this "school" closely "approaches what has been called the <u>midrash pesher</u> of the Qumran sect, in which the O.T. texts were not primarily the source of rules, but the prophecy which was shown to be fulfilled."[22] The <u>pesher</u> method is a type of running commentary on Old Testament texts in which the interpretation is woven into the text itself. In addition, an apocalyptic feature is present. The prophetic passage is viewed as fulfilled and is applied to contemporary events.[23]

Dodd's emphasis of the use by the New Testament writers of key passages and blocks of material from the Old Testament calls attention to the entire context from which the specific quotations were taken. "The relevant scriptures were understood and interpreted upon intelligible and consistent principles"[24] involving "a certain understanding of history, which is substantially that of the prophets."[25] According to Dodd, the prophets viewed history as the field upon which God continually confronted man with a challenge to which response had to be made. This response, made within certain limits of freedom, helped to shape the course of events.[26] However, the suprahistorical factor, namely, God himself, is seen as the most important influence upon history. God's impact on history is seen negatively as judgment and positively as renewal or redemption. Early Christians declared that in the death and resurrection of Jesus the act of absolute judgment and absolute redemption had taken place. Therefore, the history of God's people and of all mankind is to be understood from this central event.[27]

Ellis, who specifically attempts to determine Paul's hermeneutical methods,[28] presupposes the pesher method of quoting and interpreting and "seeks the rationale underlying the Pauline usage both in its textual manifestation and in its theological application."[29] Although there is some correspondence between Pauline and Jewish exegesis,[30] a correspondence that is to be expected since Christianity and Judaism had a similar origin, the significant conclusion is the great chasm between Pauline and Jewish exegesis. For Paul the source of the real meaning of the Old Testament lay with Christ and the apostles.[31] Much of Paul's exegesis may have its origin in the apostles who were given the key to interpreting the Old Testament by Jesus himself.[32]

Paul's exegesis was concerned mainly with the significance of the Old Testament for the Christian community.[33] Thus, his emphasis in quoting the Old Testament was upon the application of principles found in the Old Testament.[34] Two fundamental principles affecting Paul's application of the Old Testament were his understanding that Old Testament history and prophecy had been realized in Christ and his concept of corporate solidarity. By corporate solidarity is meant, for example, that "Israel the patriarch, Israel the nation, the king of Israel, and Messiah stand in such relationship to each other that one may be viewed as the 'embodiment' of the other."[35] With these considerations in mind,

Ellis is able to call Paul's exegesis "grammatical-historical plus. . . . The grammar and the historical meaning are assumed; and Pauline exegesis, in its essential character, begins where grammatical-historical exegesis ends."[36]

Vriezen indicates that Jesus' spiritual understanding of the law which sprang "from a true understanding of the heart of the Old Testament message (the love of the Holy God as the only foundation of life) and from living by this message,"[37] freed him from bondage to the letter. He showed his spiritual independence of the law in various ways. For example, he contradicted Judaic theology of his day, used the traditional text freely, and reinterpreted the meaning of the sabbath day.[38] Jesus recognized that some commandments are significant only in a certain age while others remain valid because of their purely moral and religious character.[39]

Barth describes the interpretative process used by the author of Hebrews as dialogical, christological, and pastoral.[40] Dialogical interpretation suggests the way in which the biblical text is handled. Christology is the criterion by which the text is examined and pastoral exegesis suggests what is done with the text after it is examined. Further, an application to contemporary issues is a part of exegesis.[41]

Dialogical interpretation can best be described as listening.[42] With one exception, Hebrews does not use any formula such as "it is written" to designate quotations from the Old Testament.[43] The author of Hebrews quoted from the Old Testament with reference to what was being said by it (the Old Testament) in his own time. His was a present-tense way of considering the Old Testament.[44] To quote in this way emphasized that the message was to be heard and obeyed in the first century A.D. as much as in times past.[45]

To listen to the Old Testament was to listen to what God was saying and to what was being said to God. In the Bible is revealed an intertrinitarian conversation--a dialogue between God the Father and the Son. At the same time the Old Testament reveals the triune God's concern for man,[46] and man's response to God.[47] Thus exegesis for the author of Hebrews was listening to the conversation within God and between God and man.[48] The conversation between God and man included man's response to God. Thus Barth concludes that exegesis according to the author of Hebrews was participation in the dialogue of the Bible. To this exercise only the term "dialogical interpretation" is appropriate.[49]

Participation in the biblical dialogue is neither passive nor detached. "According to Hebrews, the crucial question is whether the participant will recognize Jesus Christ . . . and give him due honor and obedience."[50] The participant must listen christologically. The participant in the biblical dialogue must listen with discernment because there are different and apparently conflicting statements in the Old Testament.[51] Just hearing the Old Testament is not enough. The exegete must weigh and evaluate the many voices and decide which are better after long and careful study. "To study the Bible means to face and collate parallel and divergent passages, earlier and later texts, and to think deeply about directions and warnings, and the contexts in which they appear."[52] To determine what is better, Jesus Christ is the spiritual criterion of the author of Hebrews.[53] This does not mean finding whatever he wants to find and neither does he find a preconceived Christology, soteriology, and eschatology.[54] The author of Hebrews attempted to elucidate the meaning of "Jesus" from the only textbook available. This required critical research in the history and literature of Israel in order to learn more about the helper of man anointed by God. That which is permanent, as distinguished from God's preliminary or transitory arrangements, is but one person, Jesus Christ.[55]

Exegesis also involves a pastoral responsibility, Exegesis is not a solitary endeavor. It is not only a personal hearing of and response to what God says in the Bible. Exegesis is also "the act of passing on the call [to obedience] to contemporaries who are living, suffering, and dying."[56] Inevitably this means making responsible decisions about contemporary issues such as world peace, atomic war, integration, and slum housing.[57]

These studies cover a broad spectrum. Some try to relate New Testament interpretative methodology to some element in the first-century historical context. Some attempt to declare that New Testament interpretative methodology was primarily different from anything in its milieu. Stendahl relates it to Qumran; Dodd to the prophets' understanding of history. Ellis begins to move away from the historical context and calls New Testament methodology christological and specifically labels Paul's methodology as grammatical-historical plus. Vriezen firmly asserts Jesus' spiritual independence while Barth declares that the personal relationship of the interpreter to God is primary.

Stendahl's finding of the pesher method of quotation emphasizes the application of the Old Testament text apart from its historical context. Although Dodd calls attention to the context of Old Testament quotations in the New Testament, his emphasis also seems to be more upon application. Ellis specifically assumes historical interpretation in his term "grammatical-historical plus" and deals primarily with theological interpretation which he calls "theological application." It is, perhaps, significant that Ellis specifically calls attention to both elements, that is, exegesis and application, in New Testament methodology when he states that his purpose is to seek "the rationale underlying the Pauline usage both in its textual manifestation and in its theological application."[58] Vriezen, likewise, seems to assume historical interpretation and stresses theological interpretation under the theme of Jesus' spiritual independence of the law. Barth is peculiarly dependent upon an existential understanding of interpretation and his emphasis is upon what is here called theological interpretation--telling "people in need of help what the Bible says of their shepherd and helper Jesus Christ."[59] However, a kind of historical interpretation with heavy existential overtones seems intended in his expression "dialogical interpretation." Further, he specifically indicates that the author of Hebrews had to do historical interpretation.[60]

The apparent finding of both historical and theological emphases in the use of the Old Testament by first-century Christians seems to support the position taken here that these two emphases are to be found throughout the history of the interpretation of the Old Testament. However, a caveat is necessary. These scholars may, to some degree, be reflecting twentieth-century thinking in their findings. If indeed New Testament interpretative methodology has both emphases there seems to be a greater emphasis on theological interpretation than on historical interpretation, on application rather than on exegesis.

## Literal Interpretation of the Old Testament

Interpretation of the Bible following the biblical period also contained the twofold emphasis of historical interpretation and theological interpretation. The historical emphasis can be seen in the literal interpretation of Marcion in the second century, the school of Antioch in the early period, the Victorines in the medieval period,[61] and the interpretation of Martin Luther. Although the emphasis of historical interpretation is apparent, these four examples of literal interpretation indicate that it certainly was not the dominant emphasis through the medieval period. Indeed, the history of literal interpretation is not continuous and forms a broken line. Marcion's emphasis, although literal, was heretical and was rejected by the Church. Both the school of Antioch and the Victorines had their "moment in the sun" and then declined to be forgotten until modern scholarship again uncovered their achievements.[62]

One writer feels that "Marcion made no real attempt to interpret the Old Testament."[63] He further asserts that the problem of second-century Christianity was solved by Marcion by simply ignoring the problem and rejecting the Old Testament as Christian Scripture.[64] However, this would seem to be a judgment of Marcion that is not totally accurate. Marcion did interpret the Old Testament and dealt with the problem of the Church's relationship with the Old Testament although both his interpretation of the Old Testament and solution of the problem were rejected by the Church as being heretical.

In his interpretative methodology Marcion rejected allegory and was largely literalistic.[65] Not only did he reject allegory in toto, he was blind to any figurative meanings.[66] He refused to believe that such passages as Ps. 72:10, 15 could refer to any except the military Messiah of Jewish expectation. Further, he believed that the promise of posterity that was made to David[67] referred only to Solomon.

In his interpretation of the Old Testament, Marcion felt that Christianity was something entirely new. He was unable to reconcile the God revealed in Jesus with the God described in the Old Testament. The God whom it truly revealed, the God of the Jews, the demiurge, was an inferior being who had created the physical world including man and ruled it on the principle of law and obedience. Further, the Messiah of the Old Testament was not identical with the Son of the true God. Thus he severed the Christian revelation from its roots.[68]

Since Marcion rejected allegory, he rejected the Old Testament because allegory was the major means in the second century for relating the Old Testament to the Church.[69] Nevertheless, one cannot say that Marcion totally rejected the Old Testament. He valued it at least as history and for its ethics. It was possibly the only history book he knew, and he accepted it as a reliable account of the past, of the earliest history of mankind and of the Jewish race, in particular, since the time of Moses. Thus, it was revelation of a kind. Further, the Old Testament was valuable as a book of ethics. He allowed the creator God to have some elements of righteousness in his character which is reflected in his book, the Old Testament. "Generally, he seems to have understood and shared the Pauline view, the paradoxical view, that though the law essentially belongs to the old order it can be described positively as holy, just, good, spiritual."[70] His attitude is revealed by significant passages in his Gospel and Apostle which he retained although they are quotations from or references to the Old Testament. Some examples are Luke 10:27; 16:29; Rom. 2:13, 20; 13:8-10; 1 Cor. 14:34.[71] Similarly, he was inconsistent in his attitude toward prophecy in general and messianic prophecy in particular. He retained some prophecies and rejected others. He allowed only two passages to refer to Jesus Christ: Mal. 3:1 and Deut. 21:23. However, this was an even greater inconsistency because he insisted that the Gospel was utterly new.

In spite of his inconsistencies and his heretical rejection of the Old Testament, Marcion did see some truths clearly. His major premise that new wine must not be poured into old bottles and his minor premise that the Old Testament is an old bottle are true. But his emphasis on the newness of the Gospel is quite exaggerated and the further inference that the old bottle is no longer needed is totally unacceptable. Some elements of his literalism are commendable, for instance, the refusal to make deductions from verses that were taken from their context. However, "it is patent that with his rigid exegetical rules he was precluded from perceiving some of the deepest truths of Scripture."[72]

All this is made vididly clear when one considers the contents of his canon. It had two main dividions: Gospel and Apostle. One gospel, a revised Luke, and ten of Paul's epistles--Galatians, Romans, 1 and 2 Thessalonians, Laodiceans which may be Ephesians, Colossians, Philippians, and Philemon--were included in Marcion's canon.[73] "Marcion . . . was committing the error of trying to possess the climax without the antecedents, which alone gave it a setting and made it intelligible."[74]

The emphasis of the school of Antioch[75] is best represented in the work of Theodore of Mopsuestia (died 429 A.D.)[76] partly because more of his work is preserved. His main work against allegory has perished but a number of his commentaries still exist. From these it becomes obvious that he attempted to interpret scripture according to the *historia*, that is, according to the literal meaning. With regard to the Old Testament, Theodore's emphasis, and his opposition to allegory, can be seen in his realization of the differences between the Old Testament and the New Testament. He understood the Psalms in their historical sense and connected them with Hezekiah and Zerubbabel allowing only three psalms to be messianic.[77] He interpreted Psalm 22 historically and applied Ps. 89:26-27 to David rather than to Christ.[78] Theodore rejected the mystic interpretation of the Song of Solomon and pointed out that it never mentions the name of God.[79] In Zech. 9:9 he rejected the allegorist method of referring in one phrase to Zerubbabel, in the next to Christ, and in the next to Zerubbabel again. Also rejected was the Alexandrian theory of inspiration which held that inspiration was a trancelike suppression of individual consciousness. The Jewish ethical idea of inspiration, which held that inspiration was the ennoblement of the individual consciousness, was more acceptable to Theodore.[80] The use of the Old Testament by New Testament writers was regarded as illustrative application rather than as proof of what the Old Testament meant.[81] One conclusion today is that "a Modern Exegete almost feels that he hears a colleague speaking when he finds such insights in Theodore."[82]

However, in spite of the Antiochene emphasis on literal interpretation and opposition to allegorical interpretation, the Antiochenes did admit more than one meaning to Scripture in the form of typology.[83]

The Abbey of St. Victor was established at Paris in 1110 A.D. The first of the three notable figures at Victor--Hugh who came to St. Victor about 1118--felt that the literal sense was the most important of three possible interpretations--literal, allegorical, typological. Two ideas helped to establish the importance of the literal sense for Hugh--his interest in history and his sacramental trend of thought which was closely linked to the historical.[84] Hugh's "great service to exegesis was to lay more stress on the literal interpretation relatively to spiritual [sic] and to develop the sources for it."[85] In addition, he was interested in studying Jewish interpretation. Jewish interpretation stimulated two of his pupils, Richard and Andrew.[86]

Andrew best represents the literal emphasis of the Victorines. In handling Scripture, Andrew's purpose was to expound select passages, and he claimed to be expounding in a historical sense.[87] "He excludes the spiritual exposition on the one hand and theological questions on the other. He has no time for homiletics or for doctrinal discussion."[88] Because he realized he was doing something new in emphasizing the literal sense, Andrew attempted to allay criticism by asserting that he was doing it for his own satisfaction.[89]

An example of Andrew's exegetical method is his treatment of the two stories of creation in

Genesis 1 and 2. He started with the text itself instead of moral and philosophical arguments, and tried to deduce the meaning of the author.[90] Another example is his treatment of the prophecy in Isa. 11:1. That which "sent other commentators instantly to the Gospel, makes Andrew think first of the prophet's reassurance to Juda [sic] and Israel."[91] In his exposition of Isa. 1:16-18 Andrew cited both pagan custom and Jewish law and tradition. His citation of Jewish tradition brings one to his chief importance as a commentator.[92]

"Jewish scholars brought the church the first dawning since the School of Antioch of central . . . interest in the literal meaning of scripture."[93] In turning to the Jews of his day for help in interpretation, Andrew was following the example set by both Jerome and his own master at Victor--Hugh.[94] Andrew's contact with Jewish exegesis was primarily oral and with Jewish rabbis living in his day. Among these were pupils of Rabbi Solomon Ben Isaac, or Rashi. The school of Rashi gave an impetus to literal exegesis among Jews.[95] It is impossible to calculate the actual extent and quality of Jewish influence on Andrew. Many of his exegetical comments are not ascribed to the Hebrews and seem to be his own work. However, "he certainly becomes a much less surprising and isolated phenomenon if we set him against the contemporary Jewish background."[96]

Although the emphasis upon the literal interpretation of Scripture was lost preceding the Reformation, there were some positive results. Andrew's emphasis upon literal interpretation "produced a crop of judaizing commentaries."[97] The evidence of Andrew's commentaries and quotations from him by later writers shows an increasing interest in his work to the end of the thirteenth century. Although the influence of the emphasis on literal interpretation in the later Middle Ages cannot be gauged accurately, Grant claims that "in the medieval claim of objectivity we find the beginning of modern scientific study of the scriptures."[98] However, the modern critical study of Scripture had to await the Reformation and the dawning of a new day--rationalism.

The Reformation began before Luther's time.[99] However, much that was involved in the Reformation, expecially as it applied to biblical studies, can be summed up in Luther.[100] Despite the diversity of Luther's interests and influences, there seems to be a kind of central ground, a focusing of energies, in his biblical studies. When he first began to lecture, he was expected to lecture on Aristotle[101] but instead determined to lecture on the Bible. He continued to lecture on the Bible the rest of his life.[102] Apparently he had his great conversion experience as a result of Bible study.[103] A lifetime of labor produced a German translation of the entire Bible and numerous editions.[104] Smart states that the Reformation was fundamentally a liberation of the Bible.[105]

It was after he began to lecture on the Bible, and especially during the years 1513-1517, that his exegetical and hermeneutical principles were molded. It is difficult to set out in specific points what his method was because it was fashioned largely as he went and in response to particular problems that he faced.[106] Ramm has adduced six principles by which, he believes, Luther was governed in his interpretation of Scripture: the psychological, authority, literal, sufficiency, christological, and law-gospel principles.[107] Whether or not all these can be substantiated as principles consciously used by Luther, these ideas certainly did affect his understanding of the Bible. In this group two stand out--christological and literal. The most important of these principles was the christological, and it permeated the others. Briefly stated, this principle means that the function of all interpretation is to find Christ.

To emphasize the christological principle does not mean a necessary de-emphasis of the literal principle. Although the former was the most important for Luther, the latter and its later influence must not be forgotten. As the authority of the Roman Church was challenged a new authority was being set up, namely, the Bible historically interpreted.[108] "The assumption of a definite, clear and consistent meaning of Scripture as a whole then becomes for Luther a cardinal point when he begins to teach that the Bible is the sole authority."[109] When literal interpretation is affirmed as a method used by Luther, due consideration must be given to Luther's background and study in scholastic interpretation. Influenced as he was by the allegorical and fourfold sense of Scripture, he at first had no problem with the unity of the Testaments.[110] Only gradually did his use of the literal principle make him aware of differences and variations in the Bible. These variations caused him to rate some books higher than others--to have a canon within a canon.[111] These variations also caused him to modify his view that Christ is to be found everywhere in the Old Testament.

His view of the relationship of the Old Testament to the New Testament is revealed in the preface to the Old Testament contained in his first edition of the Pentateuch. Basically it was the relationship of law and gospel. He stated that the Old Testament was to be highly regarded because Christ and New Testament authors so regarded it.[112] He considered the Old Testament a lawbook which taught what one should and should not do. The New Testament was a book of grace teaching where to get the strength to fulfill the law. Grace came to provide the means of fulfilling the law.[113] But in spite of the antithesis betwen law and gospel, Luther was able to find the gospel throughout the Bible and the unity of the Testaments was concentrated in Christ. "Luther sees the whole truth of the Gospel already revealed, even though veiled, in the Old Testament."[114] He made the Old Testament speak New Testament thought.[115]

The subjective realm of faith was introduced by subjecting all biblical interpretation to the christological principle. However, the Holy Spirit was important in this process.[116] If such subjective spiritual interpretation is valid, "any Christian man may read scripture under the Spirit's guidance."[117]

Some problems evident in Luther's hermeneutical methods have been set out rather clearly by Farrar.[118] It is true that faith is required to interpret the Bible. This requirement, however, must not be overemphasized.[119] It has been abused by those who were unwilling or unable to do historical and grammatical investigation. Although this is true, it would seem that without faith the layman is indeed handicapped in his ability to understand the Bible for he often has not the tools with which to do the historical-grammatical study.

Luther's rule of finding Christ everywhere in Scripture is not free from abuse.[120] Luther's view is summarized in the following statement: "I am convinced that if the Bible is to be restored to its proper place, we Christians must do it for we have the knowledge of Christ and without this, linguistic ability is nothing."[121]

Although inadequate in themselves, his exegetical principles opened the way to a sound exegesis.[122] He paved the way for a thorough literary and linguistic analysis of the Old Testament. At the same time he set a high example for anyone who would engage in such engrossing labor. There are factors in the Old Testament that patient, scholarly analysis have not solved. Luther showed that there must be room for faith in such endeavors and that such endeavors must be ultimately aimed toward the edifying of the Church. Grant states that "the correct understanding of exegesis and its task is that set forth at the Reformation by Luther."[123]

Marcion interpreted the Old Testament literally and historically. He had no room in his methodology for anything resembling the twentieth-century theological emphasis. Because of his bias against allegory, the primary methodology for obtaining a theological interpretation in his day, he was unable to relate successfully the Old Testament to the Christian scene of the second century. Marcion was right in insisting on a historical interpretation of the Old Testament. However, he was wrong in not permitting an interpretation that would allow the Old Testament to inform and influence second-century Christian life. Because he rejected allegory, Marcion did not have a means of applying the Old Testament to Christian life.[124]

The emphasis of Antioch and Victor was upon exegesis rather than application although the Antiochenes and the Victorines did not rule out the possibility of interpretations of the Scripture other than the historical. There seems to have been a recognition of the difference between exegesis and application and that application must rest upon prior exegetical work. For example, Smalley says of Andrew's work that "he excludes the spiritual exposition on the one hand and theological questions on the other. He has no time for homiletics or for doctrinal discussion."[125]

The tension between exegesis and exposition is plainly evident in Luther. Luther, in resisting the tyrannical authority of the Church, insisted on rationalistic procedures in biblical interpretation. But his insistence on making the Old Testament relevant caused him to admit to his system of interpretation the possible tyranny of subjectivism.

He was unable to combine both exegesis and exposition into a single viable system of hermeneutics. His exegesis, based on rationalistic principles, was often admirable. His exposition based on the christological principle was also admirable. However, the two were not identical.

## Allegorical Interpretation of the Old Testament

The theological emphasis in interpretation can be seen in allegorical interpretation of the Old Testament. Although the allegorical method of interpretation is generally abhorred among Bible students today, it was used and respected through much of Christian history and has long influenced Bible students, even those who specifically tried to avoid it. For instance, Luther in his attempt to return to the Bible as the seat of religious authority, particularly the Bible as interpreted according to its plain intent, had many unkind words to say about allegorical interpretation. "Yet [he] discovered meanings in the text which displayed an allegorizing ingenuity little short of caprice."[126] In finding Christ everywhere in Scripture, he read into the Old Testament the doctrines of the trinity, incarnation, justification by faith, and Reformation dogmatics.[127] In his intense reaction against allegorical interpretation, Calvin may have let it in by the back door of typology.[128] Interpreters are not above such errors today. By the measuring rod of Wolfson's definition of allegorization,[129] modern demythologizing can be called allegorization.[130]

Allegorization as a method of biblical interpretation is a descendant of Greek allegory. Greek allegory cannot be classed within the context of biblical interpretation but must be discussed when considering allegory as a method of biblical interpretation since this method was adopted by both Jewish and Christian interpreters.

Greek allegorization developed in the sixth century
B. C. in an attempt to reconcile the religious and
philosphical traditions of Greece. The literal
interpretation of the "bible" of the Greeks, the
writings of Homer and Hesiod,[131] with its fanciful
grotesque, absurd, and immoral elements, no longer
met the needs of its readers and could not be accepted by the philosphical traditions which had
developed principles of logic, criticism, ethics,
religion, and science. But the popular appeal
of these writings did not allow them to be rejected. The solution was allegorization which
made possible the finding of the best of philosophy in the unacceptable elements.[132] Homer and
Hesiod were interpreted in terms of Greek philosophy.

    Greek allegory spread to Alexandria where
there was a large Jewish population and later a
large Christian population. Alexandria became
the catalyst which promoted the growth of allegorization among both Jewish and Christian interpreters.[133] The Jewish interpreter of Alexandria
faced a problem similar to that of the Greeks.
However, "allegory was used by the Hellenists for
the totally different objects of developing out of
Moses the attenuated semblance of an alien philosophy."[134] The Jewish interpreter was reared a Jew
and wanted to be faithful to the law of Moses. In
Alexandria, he inevitably came in contact with
Greek philosophy and accepted its teachings.
While admiring Greek philosphy as inspiring and
noble, the Jew had no desire to apostatize.[135]
The tension was resolved by allegorizing the law
so that Greek philosphy could be found there.
Again, one thing was interpreted in terms of something else--the Old Testament was interpreted in
terms of Greek philosophy.[136]

    "The allegorical system that arose among the
pagan Greeks (and was) copied by the Alexandrian
Jews, was next adopted by the Christian Church
and largely dominated exegesis until the Reformation, with such notable exceptions as the

Syrian school of Antioch and the Victorines of the Middle Ages."[137] Again, allegory was the means of resolving a basic tension. The Church early adopted the Old Testament as its Scripture. Christ was the center of experience for early Christians. Since the Old Testament does not mention Christ directly, a method of interpretation had to be found which would allow Christians to find Christ in the Old Testament. To find Christ in the Old Testament required the interpreter to go beyond the surface meaning to the hidden meaning.[138]

Allegorization came to full flower in the School of Alexandria.[139] "The culmination of the allegorical method is universally acknowledged to be found in the works of Origen."[140] Origen was the first systematic theologian and produced the first thoroughgoing dogmatic work.[141] He spent the first half of his life in Alexandria and it was there that he edited his famous Hexapla and wrote First Principles.[142] Thus, it is easy to understand how he became imbued with the concepts of Hellenistic Judaism of which Philo was the outstanding representative. Origen inherited from Philo not only the allegorical system but also a love and respect for the Bible.[143]

Book IV of Origen's First Principles treats the subject of biblical interpretation. In the beginning of Book IV, Origen discusses the inspiration of Scripture. Basically he made two points in proving the inspiration of Scripture: the success of the Christian movement, predicted by Jesus, showed that it was of superhuman nature; it was the fulfillment of prophecy.[144] Then he turned to the question of interpretation. Basic to his approach was the understanding that the spiritual sense or mystical elements of Scripture had not been understood.[145]

More specifically, Origen theorized that there are three meanings in Scripture corresponding to the body, soul, and spirit, and the three degrees of perfection.[146] "The simple man may be edified by what we may call the flesh of the scripture, this name being given to the obvious interpretation; while the man who has made some progress may be edified by its soul, as it were; and the man who is perfect . . . may be edified by the spiritual law."[147] Origen was at least partially influenced by the Bible itself to come to this exegetical method. Prov. 22:20 in the Septuagint reads, "Do thou portray them threefold in counsel and knowledge, that thou mayest answer words of truth to those who question thee?"[148] The highest of these three senses or ways of interpretation, and the most edifying, was the spiritual, mystical, or allegorical. The moral sense was largely psychological and ethical. For Origen, every scripture had a spiritual or allegorical meaning while only some had the corporeal meaning. That is, while only certain statements could be taken literally, all had to be taken allegorically.

Some examples of Origen's method can be considered. Rebecca meeting Abraham's servant at the well meant, for Origen, that Christians must come daily to the wells of Scripture in order to meet Christ. While Israel was in Egypt the midwives were to kill the male children and keep the female children alive. Origen felt that the female children represented carnal affections in men and the male children represented the reasonable sense and intellectual spirit. Thus, when a man lives his life in pleasure, the male in him is being killed while the female is being preserved. When the Septuagint says in Gen. 18:2 that the three men stood above Abraham, Origen interpreted this to mean that Abraham submitted himself to the will of God.[149]

It would seem that Origen did not reduce his three general principles to more specific rules of interpretation. At least, such rules cannot be deduced from his application of allegory. His application of allegory was quite varied. However, Origen made use of several general principles which are also found in Philo. Since the Scripture is inspired by God it can never mean anything that would be unworthy of God or useless to men. The symbolism which is inherent in the Bible was used but overlaid with the symbolism flowing out of the culture of the time. He looked for allegories in the Scripture that applied to the moral life.[150]

In conclusion it can be said that Origen's intentions were admirable. His method of realizing his purpose was abominable. However, one must not forget what he owes to it and particularly to the men who employed it. The method alone is lifeless, but the spirit of the men who used it made the text of the Bible come alive for Christians in their day.[151]

The reasons why the method is lifeless can be elucidated best by defining allegorical interpretation. The definition of allegorical interpretation that is suggested by the brief review of its history is similar to the definition given by Wolfson: "The allegorical method essentially means the interpretation of a text in terms of something else, irrespective of what that something else is."[152] An additional element is implied by Wolfson, although he does not specifically add it. The "something else" which is the basis of interpretation does not necessarily have any direct relationship with the event, person, or thing being interpreted. The lack of direct relationship is stressed by both Lampe[153] and Woollcombe.[154] Further, Woollcombe stresses that allegorical interpretation seeks the secondary meaning of a text.[155] Thus, allegorical interpretation is the interpretation of a text in terms of something else which has no direct or historical relationship to it.

There is at least one other question that must be answered concerning allegorical interpretation. Is the allegorical meaning or the literal meaning the real intention of the author?

Apparently Origen felt that the allegorical meaning was the most important. Woollcombe affirms that "the main object of Christian allegorism has always been to elucidate the secondary, hidden meaning of the Old Testament, rather than to defend its primary and obvious meaning against charges of immorality."[156] However, neither Philo[157] nor Origen[158] completely rejected the literal sense or the historicity of every passage being interpreted. Philo's desire to use allegory apparently depended upon the scripture being interpreted and the purpose of the interpretation.[159] Origen reasoned similarly.

A method of interpretation such as allegory with its possibilities for going beyond the literal sense has both advantages and dangers. "It is to be welcomed so far as it frees the study of the Bible, and especially of the Old Testament, from an arid historical literalism; but it has grave dangers, dangers which were certainly not altogether avoided by the allegorists of the early and medieval Church, and of which their modern followers should be aware."[160] The danger is that it goes beyond the literal meaning with very little control over the interpretation that results except the imagination of the interpreter.[161]

As a theological interpretation aimed at applying the Old Testament to Christian life allegorical interpretation is commendable. Its de-emphasis of historical interpretation is less than commendable. Allegorical interpretation often ignored the literal or historical interpretation entirely. Further, the frequent insistence that the allegorical interpretation was the real meaning of Scripture is highly questionable because it tended to throw back upon the Old Testament ideas and attitudes which are hardly conceivable for an Old Testament personage. As application, allegory was fine and served a real need in the early days of Christianity. However, when interpreters insisted that allegory was more than application--was in fact exegesis--it became an impossible science.

There has been through the centuries a
tension in biblical interpretation between the
poles which are called here historical interpretation and theological interpretation. Interpretation in the Old Testament reveals both tendencies.
New Testament interpretation of the Old Testament
seems to lean more heavily to application. Marcion's
interpretation leaned toward historical interpretation but was quite one-sided. One could call it
extreme literalism. He recognized that the Old
Testament was not Christian on the surface and had
no means to see any elements in it that were essentially Christian. The literal interpretation of
the school of Antioch and the Victorines reveals an
attempt at moderation. Scholars in these schools
realized that the Old Testament must retain its own
character, it must remain the Old Testament, but
also must yield a Christian element. However,
neither the school of Antioch nor the Victorines
gave up allegory entirely in their insistence on a
literal interpretation. Reformation interpretation
also was subject to both emphases. Luther wanted
the Old Testament to retain its own character and
at the same time to yield a Christian element. But
he leaned so strongly toward the latter that he
tended to obliterate the Old Testament, per se, as
much as the allegorists had. The results of allegorical interpretation reveal an unbalanced interpretation but at the opposite extreme from Marcion's
literalism. Allegorical interpretation was a method to make the Old Testament Christian not only on
the surface but also in every detail. It succeeded
while, at the same time, obliterating the Old Testament as of any value in its own right. The New
Testament was so firmly impressed upon the Old
Testament that the Old Testament no longer existed
as the Old Testament. It was a New Testament prewritten.

When extreme emphasis was placed upon either
pole of the interpretative spectrum to the exclusion
of the other, such as in the case of Marcion and
Origen, interpretation of the Old Testament suffered. Thus, an adequate interpretative methodology

needs an emphasis upon both historical and theological interpretation without either becoming dominant. In addition, they must not be confused as was the case when allegorical interpretation tended to stress that the hidden meaning was the real meaning of Scripture.

¹ A history of interpretation as such will not be presented. Rather, representative methods throughout history will be discussed. John Bright (Authority, p. 57) states, "We cannot rush to solutions prematurely, as though we were the first to come at the problem. Many have wrestled with it before us, and they have much to teach us. We would do well, therefore, first of all to examine some of the solutions that have been proposed in the past and attempt some evaluation of them." In addition to substantiating the claim that Old Testament interpretation has had a twofold quality, there are other reasons why the last nineteen centuries of biblical interpretation should not be overlooked. One in particular deserves attention. If one accepts the viewpoint of Smart that the best interpretation is only relatively adequate, there will be an increasing sympathy toward the early interpreters whose methods may be considered inadequate. "In spite of the inadequacy of their methodology it is possible that they penetrated meanings in Scripture that are hidden from us, so that we can profit from the careful study of their commentaries." Smart, Interpretation, pp. 54-55.

² Carl Michalson, "Bultmann against Marcion," OTCF, p. 49; Jepsen, Essays, p. 258.

³ "Marcion and the Marcionite Churches," Encyclopaedia Britannica, XIV (1959), gives a good overall picture with a list of the most significant works on Marcion. In English see E. C. Blackman, Marcion and His Influence (London: S.P.C.K., 1948); R. S. Wilson, Marcion (London: Clarke, 1933); John Knox, Marcion and the New Testament (Chicago: The University of Chicago Press, 1942). The major work on Marcion is A. von Harnack, Marcion: Das Evangelium vom fremden Gott (Leipsig: J. C. Hinrichs, 1921 and 1924). Harnack's views were popularized by Wilson.

⁴ Gerhard Ebeling, Kirchengeschichte als Geschichte der Auslegung der Heiligen Schrift

(Sammlung Gemeinverständlicher Vorträge und Schriften aus dem Gebiet der Theologie und Religionsgeschichte, No. 189; Tübingen: J. C. B. Mohr, 1947). Cf. Gerhard Ebeling, Word and Faith, trans. by James W. Leitch (Philadelphia: Fortress Press, 1963), p. 425. A similar view is expressed by Grant, The Bible in the Church, p. 1. "The interpretation of scripture is the principal bond between the ongoing life and thought of the church and the documents which contain its earliest traditions. In past ages it has often been thought necessary to justify every doctrine of the church by explicit or implicit statements of scripture." Cf. also Wright, "The Problem of Archaizing Ourselves," p. 452. "The whole history of Christianity is in a sense the story of the constant attempt to answer this question [how does the biblical record of history become contemporary testimony?] for each generation."

[5] Since the relevance of the Old Testament for Christians must, as a matter of course, assume an Old Testament canon, this subject may not need specific consideration. However, it is important as a prelude to the New Testament understanding of the Old Testament. See Smart's emphasis on interpretation of the Old Testament, Interpretation, p. 168. He notes that four well-known histories of interpretation begin with the New Testament interpretation of the Old Testament and do not examine the Old Testament for principles of interpretation.

[6] The Reformation can be taken as a starting point, but the period since Gebler (1787) may be more significant because the rationalist influence has persisted from that time to the present. Cf. James Muilenburg, "Preface to Hermeneutics," p. 19; Grant, The Bible in the Church, p. 109.

[7] Cf. Gerhard von Rad, Old Testament Theology, Vol. II, trans. by D. M. G. Stalker (New York: Harper & Row, Publishers, 1965), pp. vii, 413.

[8] See Smart, Interpretation, pp. 170-71.

[9] Aage Bentzen, Introduction to the Old Testament, Vol. II (Copenhagen: G. E. C. Gad, Publisher, 1959), p. 212; cf. pp. 213-15. See also Smart's discussion of inspiration and revelation, Interpretation, pp. 168-71. Cf. William Hugh Brownlee, The Meaning of the Qumran Scrolls for the Bible (New York: Oxford University Press, 1964), pp. 69-83.

[10] There are several good histories of Old Testament criticism. T. K. Cheyne, Founders of Old Testament Criticism (New York: Charles Scribner's Sons, 1893); Archibald Duff, History of Old Testament Criticism (London: Watts and Company, 1910); Edward M. Gray, Old Testament Criticism (New York: Harpers, 1923); Kraeling, The Old Testament Since the Reformation; Hans-Joachim Kraus, Geschichte der Historische-kritischen Erforschung des Alten Testaments von der Reformation bis zur Gegenwart (Neukirchen Kreis Moers: Buchhandlung des Erziehungsvereins, 1956). For short summaries of biblical criticism since the Reformation, see S. J. De Vries, "Biblical Criticism, History of," IDB, I, 413-18; K. Grobel, "Biblical Criticism," IDB, I, 407-13. For a short summary of interpretation prior to the Reformation, see K. Grobel, "Interpretation," pp. 718-24.

[11] Alan Richardson, History, Sacred and Profane (Philadelphia: The Westminster Press, 1964), p. 234.

[12] See Smart, Interpretation, pp. 170-71.

[13] For a thorough discussion of these two major viewpoints, see John Bright, Early Israel in Recent History Writing, Studies in Biblical Theology No. 19 (London: SCM Press, Ltd., 1956). These viewpoints are put into practice in two significant histories of Israel: John Bright, A History of Israel (Philadelphia: The Westminster

Press, 1959); Martin Noth, The History of Israel, trans. by P. R. Ackroyd (2nd ed. rev.; New York: Harper & Row, Publishers, 1960). Cf. also the critique of the Alt-Noth approach by G. Ernest Wright, "Archeology and Old Testament Studies," Journal of Biblical Literature, LXXVII (March, 1958), 39-51. A similar disagreement on the value of history exists in the area of Old Testament theology. Cf. Eichrodt, Theology of the Old Testament, I, 512-20. He discusses his own versus von Rad's viewpoint.

[14]Technically, the use of the Old Testament in the New is a subject for New Testament studies, but, in a survey of representative ways in which the Old Testament has been used throughout history, it has a place. However, see the view of Gerhard von Rad, Old Testament Theology, II, 388.

[15]Richardson, History, Sacred and Profane, p. 234.

[16]Cf. von Rad, Old Testament Theology, II, 321. "The way in which the Old Testament is absorbed in the New is the logical end of a process initiated by the Old Testament itself."

[17]E. Earle Ellis, Paul's Use of the Old Testament (Grand Rapids, Mich.: Wm. B. Eerdmans Publishing Company, 1957), p. 1. The trend indicated here seems to parallel the trend of biblical scholarship to think in terms of the unity in the Bible. H. H. Rowley, The Unity of the Bible (Philadelphia: Westminster Press, 1953); Interpretation, V (1951), has a series of articles on the unity of the Bible that were read before the Biblical Colloquium, a group of biblical scholars and theologians sponsored by McCormick Theological Seminary; S. Vernon McCasland, "The Unity of the Scriptures," Journal of Biblical Literature, LXXIII (March, 1954), 1-10. See also below, Chapter IV, on the unity of the Bible.

[18] Such studies usually assume that the words of Jesus can be separated from those of the New Testament writer. The method and possibility of identifying Jesus' words are questions that are a part of technical New Testament research. Investigations of Jesus' use of the Old Testament have been made by W. M. Grant, The Bible of Jesus (New York: George H. Doran Company, 1927); J. W. Wenham, Our Lord's View of the Old Testament (London: Tyndale Press, 1955). Grant assumes that the words of Jesus can be separated from the words of the New Testament writer (p. 91), as does Wenham (p. 8). The same assumption is made by R. V. G. Tasker, The Old Testament in the New Testament (rev. ed.; London: SCM Press, Ltd., 1954), p. 40.

[19] Joseph Bonsirven, Exegese Rabbinique et Exegese Paulinienne (Paris: Beauchesne et ses fils, 1939); Ellis, Paul's Use of the Old Testament.

[20] C. H. Dodd, According to the Scriptures: The Substructure of New Testament Theology (London: Nisbet & Co., Ltd., 1952); Barnabas Lindars, New Testament Apologetic (Philadelphia: Westminster Press, 1961); and Krister Stendahl, The School of St. Matthew (Lund: C. W. K. Gleerup, 1954). Markus Barth, Conversation with the Bible (New York: Holt, Rinehart, and Winston, 1964), examines the use of the Old Testament in Hebrews. Lindars, whose work is primarily a textual study, presupposes the work of Stendahl, The School of St. Matthew, and Dodd. Using these prior works as a basis, Lindars examines the Old Testament quotations in the New. He believes that it is "possible to trace the history of exegetical study which has produced the forms [of the Old Testament quotations] in which they are used in the New Testament," p. 17. Although Lindars does not examine the hermeneutical aspect of the use of the Old Testament in the New per se, his work does show the importance of determining the interpretative methodology of the New Testament writers and the difficulty of doing so.

[21] Stendahl, *The School of St. Matthew*, p. 35.

[22] *Ibid*.

[23] Ellis, *Paul's Use of the Old Testament*, p. 141.

[24] Dodd, *According to the Scriptures: The Substructure of New Testament Theology*, p. 126.

[25] *Ibid*., p. 128.

[26] *Ibid*., p. 129

[27] *Ibid*., pp. 129-30.

[28] Ellis, *Paul's Use of the Old Testament*, p. 1.

[29] *Ibid*.

[30] Ellis distinguishes between exegesis and hermeneutical methods, *ibid*., p. 83, n. 4.

[31] *Ibid*., pp. 83-84.

[32] *Ibid*., p. 113.

[33] *Ibid*., p. 115.

[34] *Ibid*., p. 126.

[35] *Ibid*., p. 136.

[36] *Ibid*., p. 147.

[37] Vriezen, *An Outline of Old Testament Theology*, p. 2, n. 2.

[38] Cf. *ibid*., pp. 2-3.

[39] *Ibid*., pp. 4-5.

[40] Markus Barth, *Conversation with the Bible*, p. 235.

[41] Ibid., p. 305.

[42] Ibid., p. 213.

[43] Ibid., p. 209.

[44] Ibid.

[45] Ibid., p. 210.

[46] Ibid., p. 214.

[47] Ibid., p. 215.

[48] Ibid., p. 216.

[49] Ibid., p. 217.

[50] Ibid., p. 218.

[51] Ibid., p. 219.

[52] Ibid., p. 224.

[53] Ibid., p. 225.

[54] Ibid.

[55] Ibid., p. 226. However, Barth does not make clear the precise criteria for determining what is permanent and what is transitory.

[56] Ibid., p. 232.

[57] Ibid., p. 305.

[58] Ellis, Paul's Use of the Old Testament, p. 1.

[59] Markus Barth, Conversation with the Bible, p. 208.

[60] Ibid., p. 224.

⁶¹ Frederick W. Farrar, History of Interpretation (reprint from 1886 ed. published by E. P. Dutton, New York; Grand Rapids, Mich.: Baker Book House, 1961), p. 245, calls the Middle Ages the Dark Ages of exegesis. This is echoed by R. M. Grant, The Bible in the Church, p. 98. James D. Wood, The Interpretation of the Bible (London: Gerald Duckworth and Co., Ltd., 1958), p. 71, has a more balanced view but agrees that the Alexandrian influence was more prominent in the Middle Ages than the Antiochian. Beryl Smalley, The Study of the Bible in the Middle Ages (2nd ed.; Oxford: Basil Blackwell, 1952), p. xiii, believes that the Middle Ages was a period of creativity. "Although far less attention has been concentrated on this than on other branches of medieval studies, still, enough has been done . . . to show that the middle ages was a period of creation." Smalley is referred to extensively in discussing the Victorines since here is probably the most definitive work on biblical exegesis in the Middle Ages. Cf. the dependence on Smalley of both Wood and Grant for the period of the Middle Ages in their concise histories of interpretation. Also see P. G. Spicq, Esquisse d'une Histoire de L'Exegese Latine au Moyen Age (Bibliotheque Thomiste, XXVI; Paris: Librairie Philosophique J. Vrin, 1944).

⁶² Smalley, The Study of the Bible in the Middle Ages, p. 357.

⁶³ Wood, The Interpretation of the Bible, p. 44. See above, p. 45, n. 3, for bibliography on Marcion. Knox, Marcion and the New Testament, p. 1, n. 1, has a list of the primary sources for a study of Marcion.

⁶⁴ Blackman, Marcion and His Influence, p. 119, quoting Burkitt, Church and Gnosis (1932), p. 129, states that the real battle of the second century centered around the Old Testament. Cf. R. M. Grant, "The Place of the Old Testament in Early Christianity," Interpretation, V (April, 1951), 194-97.

See also "Marcion and the Marcionite Churches," Encyclopaedia Britannica, 1959, XIV, 868-69; Knox, Marcion and the New Testament, pp. 1-2.

[65] Blackman, Marcion and His Influence, p. 115.

[66] Ibid.

[67] 2 Sam. 7:12.

[68] "Marcion and the Marcionite Churches," pp. 868-69; cf. Henry Preserved Smith, Essays in Biblical Interpretation (Boston: Marshall Jones Company, 1921), pp. 49-50.

[69] Blackman, Marcion and His Influence, p. 116.

[70] Ibid., p. 114.

[71] Ibid.

[72] Ibid., p. 115.

[73] Edgar J. Goodspeed, The Formation of the New Testament (Chicago: University of Chicago Press, 1917), p. 187.

[74] Blackman, Marcion and His Influence, p. 120.

[75] The school of Antioch was founded in the last quarter of the third century. Robert A. Baker, A Summary of Christian History (Nashville: Broadman Press, 1959), p. 58.

[76] Farrar, History of Interpretation, p. xxxi.

[77] Ibid., p. 216; cf. Wood, The Interpretation of the Bible, p. 60.

[78] Ibid.

[79] Farrar, History of Interpretation, p. 216.

[80] Ibid., p. 217.

[81] Ibid., p. 218.

[82] Grobel, "Interpretation," p. 720.

[83] Ibid.

[84] Smalley, The Study of the Bible in the Middle Ages, pp. 89-90.

[85] Ibid., p. 102.

[86] Ibid., p. 105.

[87] Ibid., p. 120.

[88] Ibid., pp. 120-21.

[89] Ibid., p. 123.

[90] Ibid., p. 134.

[91] Ibid., p. 138.

[92] Ibid., p. 149.

[93] Grobel, "Interpretation," p. 721.

[94] Smalley, The Study of the Bible in the Middle Ages, p. 149. Cf. R. M. Grant, The Bible in the Church, p. 99.

[95] Smalley, The Study of the Bible in the Middle Ages, pp. 149-56.

[96] Ibid., p. 156.

[97] Ibid., p. 173. R. M. Grant, The Bible in the Church, p. 107, calls them "literal and historical commentaries."

[98] R. M. Grant, The Bible in the Church, p. 108.

[99] Cf. the viewpoint of Baker, A Summary of Christian History, p. vi.

[100] Smith, Essays in Biblical Interpretation, pp. 73-74; Milton S. Terry, Biblical Hermeneutics (Grand Rapids, Mich.: Zondervan Publishing House, n.d.), pp. 673-74; R. M. Grant, The Bible in the Church, p. 111. Cf. Baker, A Summary of Christian History, p. 205, "Luther . . . was the pioneer reformer that broke the power of the Roman Catholic system."

[101] Smith, Essays in Biblical Interpretation, p. 74.

[102] Willem Jan Kooinan, Luther and the Bible, trans. by John Schmidt (Philadelphia: Muhlenberg Press, 1961), p. 22.

[103] Baker, A Summary of Christian History, p. 197.

[104] George Holley Gilbert, Interpretation of the Bible (New York: The Macmillan Company, 1908), pp. 193-94.

[105] Smart, Interpretation, p. 59; Wood, The Interpretation of the Bible, p. 85; R. M. Grant, The Bible in the Church, p. 109: "It is almost a truism to say that modern historical study of the Bible could not have come into existence without the Reformation."

[106] Smith, Essays in Biblical Interpretation, p. 77.

[107] Bernard Ramm, Protestant Biblical Interpretation (rev. ed.; Boston: W. A. Wilde Company, 1956), pp. 53-57.

[108] R. M. Grant, The Bible in the Church, p. 110.

[109] Kraeling, The Old Testament Since the Reformation, p. 10.

[110] Ibid., p. 9.

111 Ibid., p. 12.

112 Kooinan, Luther and the Bible, p. 136.

113 Ibid., p. 137; cf. p. 63.

114 Ibid., p. 209; cf. pp. 213-24; Kraeling, The Old Testament Since the Reformation, p. 20.

115 Gilbert, Interpretation of the Bible, p. 202; cf. Smith, Essays in Biblical Interpretation, p. 79.

116 R. M. Grant, The Bible in the Church, pp. 112-13.

117 Ibid., p. 113.

118 Farrar, History of Interpretation, pp. 332-34. For another view, see R. M. Grant, The Bible in the Church, pp. 113-17.

119 Farrar, History of Interpretation, p. 332.

120 Ibid., pp. 333-34.

121 Kooinan, Luther and the Bible, p. 143, quoting Luther in his Preface to the OT which was published with the first edition of the Pentateuch. Cf. Kooinan, Luther and the Bible, pp. 33, 50; Gilbert, Interpretation of the Bible, pp. 197-202.

122 Smith, Essays in Biblical Interpretation, p. 81.

123 R. M. Grant, The Bible in the Church, p. 4.

124 In discussing typology Lampe states that the Church of the second century faced a dilemma: "Either the typological and allegorical method of dealing with the Old Testament, so as to make it readable as a Christian book, or the more drastic solution advocated by Marcion. Either follow such rules of exegesis as will allow the Gospel to

be read out of the Hebrew Scriptures, or throw away the Old Testament as irrelevant to those who live under the New Covenant." G.W.H. Lampe and K. J. Woollcombe, Essays on Typology, Studies in Biblical Theology No. 22 (Naperville, Ill.: Alec R. Allenson, Inc., 1957), p. 17.

[125] Smalley, The Study of the Bible in the Middle Ages, pp. 120-21.

[126] Paul K. Jewett, "Concerning the Allegorical Interpretation of Scripture," Westminster Theological Journal, XVII (November, 1954), 1.

[127] Farrar, History of Interpretation, p. 334; Johannes Geffcken, "Allegory," Encyclopedia of Religion and Ethics, ed. by James Hastings, 1908, I, 327-31.

[128] Kemper Fullerton, Prophecy and Authority (New York: The Macmillan Company, 1919), pp. 134-35.

[129] See p. 41.

[130] Richardson, History, Sacred and Profane, p. 152. Cf. Markus Barth, Conversation with the Bible, p. 273; Wright, "The Problem of Archaizing Ourselves," pp. 454-55.

[131] Ramm, Protestant Biblical Interpretation, p. 25. Cf. Harry Austryn Wolfson, Philo, Foundations of Religious Philosophy in Judaism, Christianity, and Islam, Vol. I (rev. ed.; Cambridge, Mass.: Harvard University Press, 1948), p. 131. (Hereinafter referred to as Philo.) Lampe and Woollcombe, Essays on Typology, pp. 50-51.

[132] See Smith, Essays in Biblical Interpretation, pp. 36-37; Farrar, History of Interpretation, p. 137; Wolfson, Philo, I, 131-32.

[133] Farrar, History of Interpretation, p. 138. Cf. R. P. C. Hanson, Allegory and Event (London:

SCM Press, Ltd., 1959), p. 125. After surveying
the development of allegorical tradition among
post-New Testament writers who interpreted the
Old Testament, he concludes:
> "It seems reasonable, then, to look for
> the sources of Christian allegory not
> in Alexandria but in Palestine. Its
> origins are to be traced in the ten-
> dency to see situations described in
> the Hebrew Scriptures as fulfilled
> in events of the present or of the
> immediate past, . . . in the prac-
> tice of Rabbinic allegory, . . . [and]
> in . . . Christian typology."

He defines Christian typology as "the interpreting
of an object or person belonging to the present or
the recent past as the fulfillment of a similar
situation recorded or prophesied in Scripture,"
p. 7. The "similar situation" emphasizes the
historical connection between the two events
while allegory can interpret one thing in terms
of something else without there being a historical
connection between them. Woollcombe, in Lampe
and Woollcombe, Essays on Typology, pp. 59-60,
cites the difference between Alexandrian and
Palestinian allegorization. However, the allegorical method of interpretation which has affected
Christianity for so long is more nearly Alexandrian
than Palestinian.

134 Farrar, History of Interpretation, p. 131.

135 Ibid., p. 133.

136 R. M. Grant, The Bible in the Church, p. 62.
Cf. Lampe and Woollcombe, Essays on Typology, p. 52.

137 Ramm, Protestant Biblical Interpretation,
p. 28. Cf. Wood, The Interpretation of the Bible,
p. 72.

138 Lampe and Woollcombe, Essays on Typology,
p. 52, "The main object of Christian allegorism
has always been to elucidate the secondary, hidden

meaning of the Old Testament, rather than to defend its primary and obvious meaning against charges of immorality."

139 Smith, Essays in Biblical Interpretation, p. 51.

140 Ibid., p. 52. Cf. R. M. Grant, The Bible in the Church, p. 65.

141 Hugh T. Kerr, The First Systematic Theologian: Origen of Alexandria (Princeton, N. J.: Princeton Theological Seminary, 1958). (Hereinafter referred to as The First Systematic Theologian.)

142 For an evaluation of this work as a source of Origen's thought, see Alexander Roberts and James Donaldson, The Ante-Nicene Fathers, Vol. IV (Edinburgh ed.; American reprint ed., Grand Rapids, Mich.: Wm. B. Eerdmans Publishing Company, 1953), pp. 237-38. R. M. Grant cites De Principiis and Origen's Commentary on John as "the high-water mark of allegorization in the ancient Church," The Letter and the Spirit (London: S.P.C.K., 1957), p. 104.

143 Kerr, The First Systematic Theologian, p. 12. Cf. Jean Danielou, Origen, trans. by Walter Mitchell (New York: Sheed and Ward, 1955), p. 179:
"Origen's debt to him, whether directly through the study of his writings (which we know was the case) or indirectly through Clement of Alexandria, was considerable. Philo's influence was sometimes productive of sound fruit but it also contained the seeds of serious deviation from the truth."
Parentheses his.

144 R. M. Grant, The Bible in the Church, pp. 67-68; cf. Kerr, The First Systematic Theologian, pp. 31-32.

145 Book IV.3.5, cited by Kerr, The First Systematic Theologian, p. 33.

146 Danielou, Origen, p. 188; Hanson, Allegory and Event, p. 236.

147 Book IV.2.4, cited by Kerr, The First Systematic Theologian, pp. 32-33.

148 Book IV.2.4, cited by R. M. Grant, The Bible in the Church, p. 68; cf. Farrar, History of Interpretation, p. 197.

149 Farrar, History of Interpretation, p. 199.

150 Danielou, Origen, pp. 179-86.

151 R. M. Grant, The Bible in the Church, p. 72.

152 Wolfson, Philo, I, p. 134.

153 Lampe and Woollcombe, Essays on Typology, p. 7.

154 Ibid., pp. 39-40.

155 Ibid., p. 40.

156 Ibid., p. 52.

157 Wolfson, Philo, I, 126.

158 Lampe and Woollcombe, Essays on Typology, p. 57.

159 Wolfson, Philo, I, 115-38.

160 C. H. Dodd, The Bible Today (Cambridge: University Press, 1946), p. 19.

161 Dodd (ibid., p. 18) states,
"There is . . . a sound basis for the use of the allegorical method in interpreting the Scriptures. Although it too easily

gets out of hand, yet the contrary error
of a bald and prosaic literalism may easily miss the full meaning. In the biblical
exegesis of the early Church the method
had a real value. It gave freedom from
the tyranny of already antiquated forms
of thought; freedom from the necessity
of accepting at their face value, as
part of a divine revelation, puerile
and sometimes revolting survivals from
primitive times. It gave an opening,
of which some of the finest minds took
full advantage, for a genuinely imagi-
native treatment of the Bible; and the
role of imagination in the apprehension
of religious truth should never be under-
estimated, though imagination should not
be allowed to decline into fantasy."

## CHAPTER III

## REPRESENTATIVE ATTEMPTS TO FIND THE RELEVANCE OF

## THE OLD TESTAMENT FOR THE

## CHRISTIAN FAITH: PART II

The period since the Reformation can, in general, be called the modern period in biblical interpretation and the twofold emphasis in the interpretation of the Old Testament is more evident in this period than in all the preceding centuries. Developing out of rationalism and some of the emphases from the Reformation, critical interpretation became dominant in the nineteenth century. As a reaction to some weaknesses in critical interpretation, the modern theological emphasis, that is, biblical theology, has developed strongly in the twentieth century.[1] Although Old Testament scholarship has varied from historical to theological in the recent past and although both positions at the same time have occupied biblical scholars, they may be considered separately for purposes of emphasis and clarification.

### Modern Critical Interpretation

"Modern critical interpretation" is identified here with historical interpretation.[2] The title is not intended, necessarily, to identify the latest emphasis in biblical interpretation nor to include all aspects of interpretation in the last two centuries.[3] However, the nineteenth century can, in general, be labeled the critical period.[4] Of course, there were developments which led up to the critical period, and there has been significant "carry-over" into the twentieth century.

Sometimes the roots of modern critical interpretation are found in the Renaissance, sometimes in the Reformation, sometimes in both at the same time.[5] The groundwork of such interpretation was laid by the tendency of humanistic studies to regard all ancient literature as the product of human culture and as susceptible to scholarly research on the basis of scientific principles--principles which were appled to all ancient literature.[6] At first, these principles were applied mainly to the Pentateuch. Gradually the entire Old Testament was investigated on the basis of such critical methods.

Although there were significant weaknesses in the critical approach, which will be discussed below, and the modern theological emphasis developed partly as a response to these weaknesses, the basic approach has not been negated but constantly reaffirmed even by many who contend for the theological emphasis. Smart states that "it is important in the preservation of the integrity of the Scriptures that scrupulous care should be exercised to determine as far as possible the meaning of the text in its original situation."[7] R. M. Grant affirms modern critical procedure even while calling for a theological approach.[8] No serious Old Testament student is willing to give up the critical investigative principles. A recent attempt to define some crucial issues in Old Testament interpretation candidly and forcefully presents the danger that faces the student who lacks the critical tools.[9] "The principle of objective research according to scientific methods is still the basic preliminary to Old Testament interpretation."[10]

An intergral part of critical interpretation is "the possibility and right of free investigation, free both of a not-to-be-questioned tradition and of any institution that might claim to embody and guarantee such tradition."[11] The particular type of methodology that is employed is called scientific and attempts to proceed uninfluenced by the presuppositions of any dogmatic religious tradition. The biblical materials are treated "as a body of religious literature amenable to study and appraisal by the same principles of scholarly research as were applied to any other ancient book."[12]

Various types of research are employed in critical interpretation. Grobel lists six tools of the biblical scholar: philological insight, textual criticism, literary critcism, historical criticism, form criticism, biblical theology.[13] Markus Barth describes critical interpretation under three heads: philology and textual criticism; literary criticism; historical criticism which includes three distinct sciences: archaeology, history of religion school with its comparative emphasis, and form criticism.[14] Essentially, these tools are employed in order to determine the internal and external characteristics of the biblical literature.[15] Since the Bible is literature, linguistic skills must be developed and used. After the text of this literature is restored and understood, researchers then seek to discover the style, origins, and content of the biblical materials. Thus, it is desired to learn as much as possible from a study of the literature itself, from the internal evidence. Historical research, the attempt to determine the external evidence, seeks to determine the context in which the biblical materials had their origin and life. Thus, every tool available to the historian for the discovery of the life and history of an ancient people is used.[16] With reference to the Bible, the history and milieu of the entire ancient Near East is the object of investigation.

The strengths and benefits of modern critical interpretation have given it a permanent place among the tools of biblical research. In presenting the twofold classification of interpretative methods that have been and are being used today (historical and theological interpretation) the intent is not to de-emphasize or devalue historical critical methodology. Quite the contrary is the case although historical criticism was, perhaps, pushed to an extreme in the nineteenth century, especially in the history of religion school. There were, and are, many values and benefits to historical criticism, although the development of historical interpretation has helped create the problem of the relevance of the Bible for the Christian faith.[17] "This unfortunate development, however, is not too large a price to pay for the recovery of a proper appreciation of what the Old Testament writers said in and for their day and generation, and we should be grateful for the recognition of the real diversity of thought and purpose which undoubtedly exists in biblical literature."[18] Smart makes a similar affirmation while noting the difficulty that students may have in grasping both the positive and negative aspects of modern critical research.[19]

Although credit is given to historical criticism for its many positive achievements, it is right and proper to take note of some negative aspects as well. As has already been noted above, the rise of modern historical critical study has helped to create the problem of relevance partly because of its method and partly because of overemphasis in the nineteenth century. Under the influence of Julius Wellhausen, who was the epitomy of nineteenth-century critical research, biblical scholars continued to investigate the Old Testament until criticism had almost become a goal in itself.[20] Some other weaknesses also are apparent. Critical research "failed to explain the Old Testament as a significant expression of religious aspiration"[21] and became so specialized that its view was too narrowly upon its own field. The failure of historical interpretation to accomplish its goal is further stated by Michalson.

> The most important of the problems Christians had to face in the early centuries was the question of the significance of the Old Testament. Yet the rise of the modern historical method still has not contributed substantially to a solution of those early problems. One sign of that fact is the continual oscillation between claims of the continuity of the Testaments and claims of their discon-

tinuity. Indecisiveness about the significance of the Old Testament relative to the New is as evident today as it was in the days which antedated historical science.[22]

Lampe notes that historical criticism destroyed the basis of typology, which was the unity of Scripture, and called in question the reliability of historical narratives.[23] Robert Dentan echoes the opinion that historical criticism tended to destroy the unity of Scripure when he says that fragmentation "is frequently the fruit of purely historical-grammatical studies."[24]

Another serious danger of the historical procedure is archaism. Stated in its bluntest form archaism is an attempt to live in the past in every detail. Archaism is related to the overemphasis in the nineteenth century in which history became a goal in itself.[25] Although Old Testament scholars may not necessarily be guilty of archaism, a logical conclusion of their work may lead to archaism. If the historical understanding of the Old Testament becomes the primary goal in studying and reading the Old Testament, to make it applicable to Christian life today one must attempt to place oneself in those ancient circumstances. In writing about the danger of archaism, Cadbury presents an outstanding illustration of its effect.

> A friend of mine once fell into conversation with a stranger who said he "believed the Bible from cover to cover." He admitted also that he thought the world was round and not flat. When to his surprise he was shown passages that mention the "corners of the earth" he made the consistent reply, "I begin to doubt whether the earth is round."[26]

Certainly, conscious archaism by the historian in order to gain a sympathetic understanding of the peoples and times which he studies is good and commendable.[27] When it is done consciously or unconsciously in the belief that the words and practices of another day will bring back the vital experiences of that day it is less than commendable.[28]

While recognizing the peril or problem of archaism in biblical studies one must not allow the perils to outweigh in his consideration the benefits. The direct reply of G. E. Wright to Cadbury's position helps to set the problem of archaism in perspective. Wright agrees that there is "always the danger of assuming that an ancient historical literature can simply be transplanted to a new environment without any adaptation whatever."[29] However, to say that the problem of archaism must be avoided at all costs, as does Cadbury, seems to say that the task is unimportant.[30] The attempt to interpret the Bible will always involve the problem of archaism.

Wright, who is one of the strongest proponents of the historical method, also defends it against inroads from other quarters. In contrasting his own work and his own position with reference to the Alt-Noth school in Germany, he specifically states that the historical disciplines of archeology and philology, as well as inner biblical disciplines, will be necessary to solve the problem of early Israelite history.[31] In discussing the relative merits of the form-critical approach as represented by the Alt-Noth school and its search for a cultic framework behind the patriarchal and amphityonic narratives instead of a historical framework, he says that a comparable situation in New Testament study destroyed the older quest for the historical Jesus.[32]

Wright's strong contention for the historical method is related to the idea of revelation through history although there are varied views on this subject. Wright is positively challenged at the point of revelation through history by James Barr.[33] Barr's starting point is a question which immediately casts doubt on the category revelation through history. "Is it true that the

biblical evidence, and the evidence of the Old
Testament in particular, fits with and supports
the assertion that 'history' is the absolutely
supreme milieu of God's revelation?"[34]  Barr specifically states that he is not denying any value
at all to the idea of revelation through history.
He sums up some of the values which he finds in
this category but he also pointedly notes that
revelation through history, although it has united
theology in some respects, tends to disunite because theologians cannot agree as to the nature of
the history through which revelation occurs.  Barr
also feels that revelation through history has
been and is an apologetic against the positivistic
historicism of the nineteenth century.  However,
his crucial point is that revelation through history tends to fragment the biblical materials.  In
the first place, not all materials can be subsumed
under this category.  For instance, the Wisdom
literature does not fit.  Thus, to be consistent,
Wisdom has to be elminated in subsuming biblical
materials under this category.  In addition, there
are aspects of the crucial historical materials
which are usually appealed to in discussing revelation through history which do not fit under
this category either.  For instance, in the exodus
story and surrounding events there is an element
of revelation through the direct word of God to
Moses.  God spoke to Moses directly, not through
a historical event.  Therefore this element has to
be eliminated when subsuming biblical materials
under the category of revelation through history.[35]

If Barr's idea of direct verbal communication from God to men is coupled with the idea
of revelation through history, then there will be
something of a word-event-interpretation complex
and this would justify the need for re-interpre-
tation of the revelatory message in each new age.
James Smart feels that sometimes in the emphasis
on revelation through history (or events)

> the fact is lost from sight that in both
> Testaments the event is always an inter-
> preted event.  Event (sic) in history and

interpretation are inseparable, so that
the event without the interpretation would
not be a revelation to anyone.[36]

Smart commends Wright's emphasis on events but takes a stance similar to Barr's position.[37]

Although Barr's major contention (the category of verbal communication[38] between God and man must also be considered in addition to revelation through history) is not equally acceptable to all theologians, it seems apparent that, in general, his position is correct. Other categories than revelation through history need to be considered when dealing with the biblical materials. If this is true, then other methods of interpretation than the historical, or methods which extend the historical, may be needed in order to understand adequately and fully the message of God contained in the Bible. Theological interpretation is an attempt to provide other methods of interpretation.

## Current Theological Interpretation

Current theological interpretation, biblical theology, [39] has roots reaching back almost as far as the roots of modern scientific interpretation. Smart, in chronicling the "death and rebirth of Old Testament theology,"[40] states that Old Testament scholarship has been consistently untheological in the recent past (with an overemphasis on historical interpretation) giving the impression that this attitude belongs per se to the critical approach to the Scriptures. But this untheological character developed not in the first but in the second period of modern critical investigation of the Old Testament. In the first period, in the eighteenth and early nineteenth centuries, crictical scholars held "that the Old Testament constitutes a necessary part of the record of the revelation from which the church draws its life."[41] Early in the nineteenth century critical scholars substituted a critical and historical approach for an uncritical. Eichhorn,

DeWette, Ewald, Vatke, Delitzsch, all honored names in the first period of critical scholarship, "took it as in the nature of their responsibility to be theologians of the Christain church as well as linguistic and historical scholars."[42] Oehler, Dillmann, and Schultz continued this tradition in the latter part of the nineteenth century. Therefore the suggestion that the Old Testament scholar has a theological responsibility is not a new demand but a return to an old and honorable tradition. Today's conception of Old Testament science limits "it to an objective presentation of the literature, the history, the culture, and the various phases of religious development of the ancient people of Israel."[43]

It was inevitable that this purely historical character of Old Testament science should develop in reaction to the unsatisfactory method of the first period, but this development has possibly neglected "some principles which were at work in that primary period and which are necessary to the preservation of a healthy Old Testament scholarship in the church."[44]

Among the many emphases in biblical theology today, only a few can be examined. As diverse as some of these emphases are, they have one common element. They attempt to do justice to the spiritual element in Christianity and biblical interpretation without abandoning the critical principles which biblical scholars in general accept. In this they are attempting to make the Old Testament relevant to the modern scene.

Muilenberg presents five methods which he says are attempts "to overcome the embarrassments of historical relativism."[45] The first he mentions is the viewing of history as a unilinear development which had the disadvantage of "ignoring other lines of movement and of neglecting such portions of the Bible as do not cohere with this treatment."[46] The others are typology, which is especially represented by von Rad's efforts, representation, which is associated with Martin Noth, existentialism, and christological, which recalls the work of Wilhelm Vischer. Hummel believes that "there are currently two main stresses concerning the unity of the testaments: typology and sensus plenior."[47] Again, von Rad is associated with the former and Roman Catholicism with the latter. In reducing the major emphases to two in number, Hummel has incorporated some other emphases. "In one way or another, prophecy-fulfillment, Heilsgeschichte, and Christological approaches tend to merge with both of these major stresses."[48] Markus Barth cites Bultmann's existentialism, the Roman Catholic doctrine of sensus plenior, and von Rad's typology as alternative approaches to the problem of hermeneutics that are presently receiving scholarly attention.[49] Filson goes further in listing new approaches to the interpretation of the Old Testament. Among the methods he cites are unity-of-ideas, allegory, law and gospel, promise and fulfillment, typology, homology, existentialism, various views of history.[50] Carl Braaten singles out four lines of theological approach to the biblical materials: the christological, existential, typological, and historical.[51] Obviously there is considerable overlapping in what is considered important as a major emphasis in current theological interpretation. But to serve the purpose of examining representative attempts to find the relevance of the Old Testament, three of these methods will be presented here: typology, sensus plenior, and existentialism.

## Typology[52]

There is a current revival of interest in typology among the biblical scholars, especially in Germany and Great Britain. A renewed emphasis on the unity of the Bible[53] as a whole "and on the supposition of a common pattern to which every book of the Bible contributed its share"[54] has been the main reason for this revival. Other concommitant reasons can be given.[55] New interest has been shown in the New Testament use of the Old

Testament. Some features of this use of the Old Testament are unique to the Christian movement—the emphasis upon promise and fulfillment; the association of events in the New Testament with corresponding events in the Old Testament. A pattern of correspondences in events—past, present, and future—has been recognized in the Old Testament itself. Increasingly it has been recognized that a Christian interpretation of the Old Testament must be in some definite way christological. Also there has been a renewed interest in the commentaries of Luther and Calvin in which the Bible is allowed to speak its message to Christians with theological penetration. Above all, the whole trend of biblical theology which has sought to alleviate the barrenness of purely historical exegesis has contributed not only to a renewed emphasis on typology but on other theological interpretations also.

The revival of interest in typology has not been without strong doubts and apprehensions about its appropriateness. Typology and allegory, which have been closely associated in the history of interpretation, have often led to extremes of interpretation and abuses which the emphasis upon historical interpretation largely overcame. A return or even the possibility of a return to those abuses is not looked upon favorably by biblical scholars. However, most of the scholars who are interested in typology as a legitimate method of interpretation are also committed to historical interpretation. For instance, Smart lists A. G. Hebert, G. W. H. Lampe, Wilhelm Vischer, and Karl Barth as fully committed to the historical character of Scripture.[56] Other names can be added to Smart's list, among them von Rad who voices a warning against separating typological interpretation from historical interpretation.[57]

In the renewal of interest in typology there has been a significant debate on the continent between Martin Noth and Gerhard von Rad on the one hand and A. A. van Ruler and Friedrich Baumgartel on the other hand. The debate illustrates the difficulty which some scholars have in accepting typological interpretation as valid.[58] Noth and von Rad affirm the possibility of typological interpretation while van Ruler and Baumgartel reject it altogether.

Van Ruler rejects typological interpretation because many promises are apparent in the Old Testament and he feels Christ cannot be the fulfillment of all of them. Similarly he sees in the Old Testament many ways of reconciliation while in the New Testament there is only one.[59] Thus one should not expect to find correspondences between the Old and New Testaments.

Baumgartel rejects typological interpretation because he feels it ignores and does not adequately treat the religious experiences of Old Testament people as time-bound.[60] That is, the "inner structure of the pious existence of the Israelites . . . is not our understanding."[61] It belongs to another time. Baumgartel insists that the Old Testament remain Old Testament. "Its witness does not come out of the gospel, but out of a religion which lived under different historical and religious conditions. With this recognition, the typological and Christological methods of interpretation fall."[62] The "once-for-all-ness" of Old Testament events is emphasized by Baumgartel so strongly that there is no room in his procedure for the possibility of a correspondence between events that are separated in time.

Von Rad, on the other hand, emphasizes just as strongly the correspondences which he believes exist between events that are separated in time. For von Rad the Old Testament is dominated by a form of typological thinking that emphasizes "the eschatological correspondence between beginning and end."[63] Von Rad feels such correspondences are "an elementary function of all human thought and interpretation."[64]

Noth, rather than speaking directly of typology, speaks of the possibility of re-presen-

tation in which past events are contemporized in
certain details by retelling them.[65] The basis
for re-presentation is that "God and his action
are always present, while man in his inevitable
temporality cannot grasp this present-ness except
by 're-presenting' the action of God over and over
again in his worship."[66]

The history of typological interpretation
has not been smooth. Lampe states, "Nowhere do the
changes which have come over our reading and understanding of the Bible find more striking expression than in the different attitudes which
have been adopted towards the typological and
allegorical methods of interpreting the Scriptures."[67] Lampe describes the history of typology
in three steps. Before the rise of modern critical study a person reading the Bible "found a
coherent pattern running through every part of
Scripture."[68] The Bible was a unity. Events and
prophecies in the Old Testament were valuable
primarily for what they foreshadowed.[69] With the
rise of modern critical study the chain of continuity in the Bible was broken. The ancient writers
were understood as speaking to their own time and
not a later time in type and allegory. "Typologiz-
ing . . . came to a sudden end in rationalism."[70]
However, the recent emphasis on the unity of the
Bible has again created an interest in typology.

Typology has been used for various purposes
among biblical interpreters. Darbyshire notes
three ways in which typology has been used. In
each case excesses have occurred. His first group
consists of those who used types for apologetic
purposes--for instance, Justin and Origen. Justin
used the Old Testament as a source of teaching
about Christ in order to reach the unbelieving
Jews by whom the Cross was despised. Second, some
interpreters such as the successors of Origen and
Clement at Alexandria attempted to use typology for
edification. In the third group Darbyshire places
the Scholastics of the Middle Ages who used typology constructively. By "constructive" he means
that they used typology to buttress their theologi-

cal systems.[71] The occurrence of excesses in the use of typology by many in the past is ample reason for the apprehension today concerning the interest in typology among some biblical scholars. The excesses also point to the need to clarify explicitly what is meant by typology and the limitations placed upon it in order to insure against excesses in the future.

One such limitation and a basic presupposition with which biblical interpreters begin when attempting to defend and explicate the new typology is the historical sense of Scripture. Historical interpretation must precede and be the foundation for any typological interpretation. A second presupposition and the real basis for any typological interpretation is a particular kind of relationship that is alleged to exist between the Old and New Testaments. As stated by Markus, this relationship hinges on what the New Testament writers saw in the Old Testament.[72]

The attempt to define the particular relationship between Old and New Testaments and to make use of it in biblical interpretation has often led to allegory. However, those who advocate most strongly the validity of typological interpretation insist that there is a definite distinction between typology and allegory. They insist that allegory is wholly subjective[73] while typology is concerned with the literal sense, "although not so much with the actual words as with the events, persons or institutions they describe."[74] Woollcombe makes a similar distinction between typology and allegory.

> Typological exegesis is the search for linkages between events, persons or things <u>within the historical framework of revelation</u>, whereas allegorism is the search for a secondary and hidden meaning underlying the primary and obvious meaning of a narrative. This secondary sense of a narrative, discovered by allegorism, does not necessarily have

any connexion at all with the historical framework of revelation.[75]

In defending typological interpretation a further distinction is sometimes made between typology and promise-fulfillment. Since typology deals with "linkages between the Old and New Testaments, it is akin to the study of the fulfillment of prophecy."[76] The stated distinction between typology and fulfillment of prophecy is that the latter term should be used to describe only those instances in which there is a literal fulfillment of the Old Testament in the New.[77]

If typology is neither allegory nor fulfillment of prophecy, what is it? Woollcombe defines it as exegesis and as a method of writing. As a method of exegesis it is the establishment of historical connections between events, persons, or things in the Old Testament and similar events, persons, or things in the New Testament. As a method of writing it is the use for descriptive purposes of terms borrowed from the Old Testament.[78] In addition, Woollcombe strongly emphasizes that the linkages between events, persons, or things is "within the historical framework of revelation."[79] Similarly, Lampe defines typology as a method of study "which seeks to discover and make explicit the real correspondences in historical events which have been brought about by the recurring rhythm of the divine activity."[80]

Von Rad, in several statements, sums up his view of typology. Typological interpretation will go beyond the historical interpretation but will not be separated from it. Although the number of Old Testament types is unlimited,

> typological interpretation has to do only with the witness to the divine event, not with such correspondences in historical, cultural, or archaeological details as the Old Testament and the New may have in common. It must hold itself to the kerygma that is intended, and not fix

upon the narrative details with the aid
of which the kerygma is set forth.[81]

Typological interpretation is aware that the redemptive benefits of the Old Testament do not equal those of the New Testament but foreshadow eternal salvation. In using typological interpretation the interpreter is not compelled to find in the Old Testament text a hidden meaning, "some truth beyond that inherent in the event itself."[82]

Terminology in interpretation tends to produce some of the problems with which interpreters must wrestle. Perhaps typological interpretation is more sensitive at this point than some other methods because of its close association with allegory. Von Rad seems to prefer the terms analogy or correspondence. "One must see the basic ideas of typology less in the notion of 'repetition' than in that of 'correspondence.'"[83] Markus attempts to set forth principles to guide interpreters in determining the "sense of Scriptures" because he believes a lack of clarity about principles has resulted in a confusion in terminology.[84] Lampe also prefers to emphasize the correspondences between the Old Testament and the New Testament.[85]

Both dangers and benefits accompany the use of typological interpretation. Perhaps the most obvious danger, at least the most persistent through the history of typological interpretation, is that typology slips so easily into allegory where the historical meaning of a text is not really taken seriously.[86] Smart has called attention to the recognition of this danger by several Old Testament theologians who are interested in a kind of typological interpretation.[87] In rejecting typology as a proper method of interpretation for the modern interpreter, Wright strongly emphasizes the tendency of typology to slip into allegory and to ignore the historical context. Wright also adds that there is an even more serious danger in a static approach to the Bible such as typology. It achieves the same end as allegory without being so openly unhistorical. Although the truth sought is ostensibly linked to its historical context, it is in reality an eternal truth much like the Greek search for eternal verities.[88] With these strictures against typological interpretation, Wright warns against erecting a systematic hermeneutics based on typology.[89]

However, in spite of the dangers and the rejection of typological interpretation by many Old Testament scholars, scholars who advocate typology insist that in a carefully controlled use of this interpretative method there are certain very real and valuable benefits. According to Wolff, typological interpretation can aid both the Old Testament exegesis and the church's proclamation. First typology can serve as a heuristic aid in determining what the Old Testament is really talking about. Also, typology can promote the investigation of intention in the explanation of a text. "The constant consideration of the New Testament *eschaton* helps the expositor to interpret the Old Testament text in a way that is true to the material, in a forward direction, in the direction of the actual witnessing intent of the texts in their contexts."[90] Typology can help produce theological solidarity in regard to "the witnessing intent of the Old Testament, and warns the expositor against finding too quickly in the Old Testament texts testimony to a God who is foreign to the Father of Jesus Christ."[91]

Wolff's statements regarding the way in which typology can aid the church's proclamation center around the historical element. Since many Old Testament texts witness to the will and purpose of Israel's God, a typological consideration "brings us above all to the insight that it is God who is at work in Jesus Christ."[92]

In spite of the possibilities of helpfulness in the typological method, some strictures must be voiced. First, even granting the highest intentions to those who advocate this method, there is still a strong tendency and possibility of reading back from the New Testament into the Old Testament. For instance, Wolff gives several examples of what he means by heuristic aid, among them the following. "How could there have been for so long those stiff-necked misinterpretations in the exposition of the laws in the Pentateuch if the analogy of the Pauline exhortations or of the Sermon on the Mount had been used as heuristic aids in discovering the state of affairs in the Old Testament?[93] Second, and more importantly the claim is patently made that typological interpretation is, at one and the same time, an aid both to critical research and to proclamation. Wolff states the first point explicitly.[94] The second point is made just as strongly.

> If the essential presupposition of typology is correct, that the Old Testament does not bear witness to a strange God, but to the Father of Jesus, then it must be allowed to speak completely with the kerygma that is its own. But then typology does not lead only to historical understanding, but also at the same time to an exposition of the Old Testament that is proclamation, in as far as the God of Israel is the God of the church, is God today, in as far, therefore, as the character of the Old Testament as address is also relevant to us.
> . . . . . . . . . . . . . . . . . . . . . . . .
> Typology . . . knows it can deal properly with the Old Testament only by practicing exposition which is historical, which compares the Old Testament with the New, and which is thus proclamation.[95]

Whether the typology advocated above is valid or not is a question that cannot be answered here. However, taking at face value its claims that it is an aid to understanding the religious (or theological) context of the Old Testament, it is more closely related to historical hermeneutics than to theological hermeneutics. As such it is an asset to biblical scholarship which is to be welcomed. But when it claims to be both historical interpretation and theological interpretation at the same time, confusion results because the differences between historical hermeneutics and theological hermeneutics tends to be obliterated and the real nature of theological interpretation as application is obscured.

## Sensus Plenior

Sensus plenior is a method used primarily by Roman Catholic interpreters.[96] It has been carefully defined and defended by Raymond E. Brown.[97] In general usage the term sensus plenior means any more profound interpretation of the Bible. As a specific title of a sense of Scripture it is of rather recent vintage, dating back to about 1920. However, there was a precedent for such a classification as early as the nineteenth century.[98]

Because sensus plenior is closely linked to literal and typical senses of Scripture, it is advantageous to define these senses at the outset. The literal sense is that which was clearly intended by the human author.[99] The intention of the divine author leads into sensus plenior. The literal sense is the "meaning which the human author, inspired by God, wanted to express."[100] The typical sense is the sense of things. Something "about which the text of Scripture speaks literally is used by God to fore-shadow something else."[101]

Brown gives the following as a working definition of sensus plenior. "The sensus plenior in that additional, deeper meaning, intended by God but not clearly intended by the human author, which is seen to exist in the words of a Biblical text when they are studied in the light of further revelation or development in the understanding of revelation."[102] Although the human author did not clearly intend this meaning, it can be called a sense of Scripture since God is the principle author of the Bible and it was intended by God. Brown says that all scholars would concede that the human author did not clearly intend the fuller sense.[103] The extent of his intent, however, is greatly disputed. The fuller sense exists in the words of the text. It is not a typical sense or a sense of things written about in the text. The fuller sense is already present or latent in the text and thus presupposes the literal sense.[104] A legitimate sensus plenior must have a very real connection to the literal sense.[105]

Four proofs of this definition are given by Brown. The exegesis by the New Testament writers and the Fathers was more than literal yet not exclusively typical. The exegesis by the liturgy and of certain Marian texts by theologians is not literal and neither is it typical. Yet the more profound meaning flows from the text itself. Finally, this definition aids in harmonizing the two Testaments. It shows that the New Testament is an outgrowth of the Old Testament and is the fulfillment of the destiny of Israel. Of this, Brown says that the deeper meaning of the Old Testament text was made clear in later times. The sensus plenior classifies exactly such a meaning.[106]

After defining sensus plenior and giving the proofs of this definition, Brown then gives a more precise division of the term: general sensus plenior, typical sensus plenior, and prophetical sensus plenior. General sensus plenior simply means that the totality better helps one understand the parts.[107] Brown confines general sensus plenior to historical developments.[108] The typical sensus plenior is more difficult to explain since the typical sense of Scripture is one of the major senses of Scripture. Brown defines it with an example. There were things in the life of David which foreshadowed Christ. That is, David was a type of Christ. These things in David's life are expressed in certain biblical passages. However, there are other words from David which have nothing to do with the things in David's life which foreshadowed Christ but nevertheless find a fuller meaning in Christ, for example, Psalm 2. Nevertheless, the fact of a fuller sense in Christ is due to the circumstance of David being a type. Therefore, the division typical sensus plenior is a proper one.[109] The prophetical sensus plenior is the meaning which a prophecy is seen to possess once it has been fulfilled. For instance, many

Old Testament prophecies were understood fully only when Christ came.[110]

As stated above, sensus plenior is related to the literal sense and typical sense of Scripture. The relationship to the literal sense depends upon the definition of the literal sense and upon whether one allows the writer any knowledge of the fuller sense. Brown prefers to limit the literal sense to that which was clearly intended by the human author. Thus, sensus plenior is not strictly speaking a literal sense.[111] In saying that the sensus plenior is not strictly speaking a literal sense, Brown takes great care to leave room for the biblical writer to have some knowledge of the fuller sense of which he was writing. "It is worth noting that the lack of clear awareness may run all the way from absolute ignorance to near clarity."[112] Brown illustrates this relationship by speaking of seeing a room in the very dim light of evening and then returning to it in the bright light of day. "Nothing has been changed; nothing new has been added" but now we see all the furniture and paintings clearly where before we could just make out the dim outline."[113]

Although both the typical sense and the typical sensus plenior were not within the clear knowledge of the human author, Brown makes the distinction that the typical sense is primarily a sense of things while the sensus plenior is is primarily a sense of words. However, clear separation or complete correlation of the two is not always possible. There are many borderline cases.[114] In conclusion, Brown says that the sensus plenior

> is a distinct sense from either the literal or the typical, holding a position between the two, but closer to the literal. Like the literal sense, it is a meaning of the text; unlike it, it is not within the clear purview of the hagiographer. It shares this latter character-

istic with the typical sense; but unlike the typical sense, it is not a sense of "things" but of words. In practice, there will be many borderline instances in both directions where it is impossible to decide just what sense is involved.[115]

Some scholars raise certain objections to the sensus plenior. Brown undertakes to answer these objections. First, the new meaning which constitutes the sensus plenior does not come from within the text but is added on by new revelation.[116] The idea in this objection is that the Old Testament presents a gradual development of revelation. To read more into Old Testament texts than the author clearly intended is to do so by virtue of an increased knowledge of revelation not because such a fuller meaning was actually in the tex in the first place. Brown's answer is that when God gave a partial revelation, it was pedagogic. That is, God was at the same time preparing his hearers for the fullness of that revelation.[117] Further, the Hebrew language is peculiarly adaptable to carrying such hidden meanings.[118]

A second objection to the sensus plenior is that by classifying it as "an homogenous development of the literal sense, one distends and overstuffs the literal sense, and opens the way for abuses."[119] Brown firmly asserts here that the determination of the literal sense is the first duty of exegetes. Therefore, this charge is not unimportant. He answers, however, by saying that separating the sensus plenior from the literal sense and yet relating it to the literal sense removes the objection.

A third objection is that the sensus plenior is not a scriptural sense at all since the human author was unconscious of it. To answer this objection, Brown goes back to his precise definition of sensus plenior. That is, the sensus plenior was intended by God. The human author was merely the instrumentality of this intention. "God is, after all, the principle Author of

Brown's view of the unity of the Testaments seems to relegate the Old Testament to a merely pedagogic function.[131] Further, Brown's answer to the first objection which he himself raises makes clear that he has room in his thinking for a kind of progressive revelation in which fuller revelation comes later in time.[132] If revelation develops in this way, then one could assume that continuing revelation is presenting Christians in every age with fuller revelation. The logical conclusion is that the former revelation is not needed after the fuller revelation is known.[133]

## Existentialism

In any discussion of existential hermeneutics as it applies to the Bible, the concepts and procedures of Rudolf Bultmann must be considered. For Bultmann the character of Old Testament religion is apparently different than New Testament religion. He affirms that

> our history is the basis for a demand of the Old Testament upon us. . . . This demand, however, is completely different from what the New Testament and the Christian church attribute to the Old Testament when they designate it as <u>revelation,</u> as God's Word.[134]

In the Old Testament existence under the law was thought of as grace but it was grace only in connection with a particular history and a particular people.[135] The individual experienced grace as God dealt graciously with Israel.[136] However, because of Christ the grace of God is no longer tied to a particualr people and a particular history. "God's grace is forgiveness pure and simple."[137]

Bultmann's discussion of prophecy and fulfillment perhaps can clarify the difference which he sees between the Old Testament and the

New Testament. For Bultmann the Old Testament does not speak directly of Christ. Therefore, the New Testament intent to find in the Old Testament messianic prophecies which directly predict Christ had to be accomplished by allegorizing. Bultmann accuses New Testament writers of taking what is already known, Christ, and reading it back into the Old Testament.[138] "This method of finding proohecy abandons the text of the Old Testament to the mercy of arbitrary choice, and the grotesque examples in the apostolic fathers are simply the consequence of the method of the New Testament authors."[139]

Since the Old Testament does not speak directly of Christ, can it stand at all as prophecy which points toward a fulfillment? After examining three ideas found in the Old Testament--the covenant concept, the concept of the kingdom of God, and the concept of the people of God--Bultmann concludes that they are concerned with an empirical dimension within the world.[140] and that this empirical dimension is not able to contain all that is meant by the concepts. This leads toward a transcendent God and his activity.[141] "The idea of a covenant of God with a people shows itself to be an impossible development within history and becomes an eschatological idea."[142] Bultmann calls this a miscarriage of history because historical development whould not lead to the eschatolgical idea. Historical development in the Old Testament leads to an impasse. Thus, Old Testament history is a history of failure.[143] In other words, Christ is not the end result of a developmental process. One cannot, according to Bultmann, see Christ as the goal of history by looking forward through history. Only by looking backward can Christ be seen in this way.[144] Thus, Christ is not directly predicted in the Old Testament.

For Bultmann, Christ is the beginning of a new dimension and cannot be the fulfillment of something of which he was not a part. In the New Testament Christ is the end of salvation history not in the sense that he signifies the goal of historical development, but because he is its eschatological end.[145] However, since Old Testament history comes to an impasse, a miscarriage, a failure, it may be regarded as prophecy and therefore promise in the sense that in its failure it points to something better. "This miscarriage (of history) is, of course, to be understood as a promise only on the basis of its fulfillment, that is, on the basis of the encounter with God's grace, which makes itself available to those who understand their situation as one of impossibility."[146] That is, man must know himself to be in an impossible situation in order to see the way out through God's grace. God's grace, then, can be regarded as promise to the impossible situation of man's existence. Thus, the New Testament, Christ, stands as promise to the impasse of Old Testament history although the fulfillment is in a new eschatological dimension.

For Bultmann, then, the Old Testament is regarded as pedagogically advantageous for Christianity. It can teach man the impossibility of his situation and the necessity of turning to Christ. That is, the value of the Old Testament for Christianity is pedagogic and not instrinsic.

In addition to viewing the Old Testament and New Testament as different on the basis of historical development, Bultmann also feels that Christianity contains another element that is specifically Christian and is not included in Old Testament religion. A basic characteristic of the New Testament is that man's relation to God is bound to the person of Jesus.[147] The Church proclaimed him and bound the God-man relationship to his person.

However, Bultmann insists that Christianity must retain the Old Testament.[148] The Old Testament presents an understanding of human existence which can be valuable to the Christian. In dialogue with the Old Testament, what can be learned about what man is and how he is to exist?[149] The understanding of existence in the Old

Testament calls man not to an idealistic concept of human personality nor to a flight into timelessness where concrete history becomes an illusion. Man "is directed into his concrete history with its past and future, with its present that lays before him the demand of the moment in concrete relation with the 'neighbor.'"[150] This understanding of existence is the same as that of the New Testament and is, therefore, not just an isolated case in which a particular understanding of existence is exemplified. Rather, it stands as a part of man's own past and, thus, man's own "history is the basis for a demand of the Old Testament upon us."[151] Thus, Christianity must retain the Old Testament or the Christianity man has is no longer Christianity.

However, other materials can also instruct man in this way. "The pre-understanding of the Gospel which emerges under the Old Testament can emerge just as well within other historical embodiments of the divine law."[152] The demands which the Old Testament makes upon man are truly moral demands and do not arise out of the concrete, cultural, national, and social conditions of a certain period. Rather, they spring out of human relationship. They are, therefore, not specifically Old Testament demands and are validated for man not just by the Old Testament but because they are grounded in human relationship. Every period finds them simply by serious reflection upon this relationship. Further, they are not found exclusively in the Old Testament.[153] Thus, it is only for pedagogical reasons that the Christian Church uses the Old Testament to make man conscious of standing under God's demand.[154] For Bultmann, this is not the same as revelation. That is, the Old Testament is not God's Word.[155] "Critical, historical reflection and response to the demand of our own history is not hearing the Word of God and is not faith."[156] Bultmann evidently feels that God's grace when mediated by historical circumstances is not in fact revelation. In the Old Testament God's grace was operative primarily because he had given Israel her history as a history of salvation.[157] Grace was experienced by individuals as God dealt graciously with Israel.[158] In the New Testament God's grace is no longer tied to a particular people and a particular history. "God's grace is forgiveness pure and simple."[159] Of course, Jesus Christ is the focus of this grace.

> In the New Testament, God's deed in Jesus Christ is not understood in the same way (as in the Old Testament); it is not a historical event that is decisive by the history of Israel, so that by virtue of historical solidarity every later generation receives the benefit of what Jesus meant to this generation. Jesus cannot be remembered like Abraham or Moses.
> . . . He is the eschatological deed of God which makes an end of all ethnic history as the sphere of God's dealing with man.
> . . . The message of the forgiving grace of God in Jesus Christ is not a historical account about a past event, but rather it is the Word which the Church proclaims, which now addresses each person immediately as God's Word and in which Jesus Christ is present as the "Word." For in this word the individual is confronted immediately by God, God's forgiving grace. He is not to look to demonstrations of God's grace fround in historical events of the past, deducing from them that God is gracious and accordingly may also be gracious to him; rather God's grace confronts him directly in the proclaimed Word.[160]

Thus, for the Christian the Old Testament, the history of Israel, is not history of revelation. "So far as the Church proclaims the Old Testament as God's Word, it just finds in it again what is already known from the revelation in Jesus Christ."[161] By Bultmann's reasoning the Old Testament is not Christian Scripture and is basically unnecessary. He has been accused of Marcionism for his viewpoint.[162] However, he does retain the Old Testament as pedagogically valuable for

Christianity.

Bultmann insists that if the Church uses the Old Testament in its proclamation then it must use the Old Testament in its original sense.[163] Further, he insists that the Old Testament be used "only in so far as it is actually promise--that is, preparation for the Christian understanding of existence. To this extent one may say that Christ already speaks in the Old Testament."[164] By the second restriction much of the Old Testament would hardly be usable by the Church because much, if not all, of it is historically bound and is concerned with an empirical dimension within the world. Also, the second provision allows the Old Testament to be no more valuable for Christianity than other historical sources which can also prepare for the Christian understanding of existence.

Bultmann evidently would interpret the Old Testament in the same manner that he describes for the New Testament--an existential form of interpretation.[165] In one sense exegesis must be without presuppositions. It must not presuppose the results of the exegesis. Thus allegorical interpretation is ruled out, and exegesis must not be guided by prejudice.[166] However, in another sense exegesis does have presuppositions. For instance, the historical method of interrogating a text is presupposed.[167] Further, the historical method presupposes that "history is a unity in the sense of a closed continuum of effects in which individual events are connected by the succession of cause and effect."[168] This means that all events have a relationship of cause and effect and the task of the historian is to discover by means of the historical method the causes or the motives of events in order to exhibit them and their connection. In seeking to understand a text, in seeking to understand the causes that connect the individual historical phenomena, every historian assesses these connecting factors in a specific way. "The individual historian is guided by some specific way of raising questions, some specific perspective."[169] In addition, as the historian attempts to understand the phenomena themselves, that is, the subject matter, a pre-understanding or life-relation is presupposed. The interpreter already has a relation to the subject expressed in the text. The historical picture is falsified by this only if the exegete regards his pre-understanding as the only possibility, as a definitive understanding. Only by having such a prior relationship to the subject in the text can an interpreter hope to understand history. "We speak of this encounter with history that grows out of one's own historicity as the existentiell encounter. The historian. participates in it with his whole existence."[170] This understanding of history is not subjective. It means that the phenomena of history are only understandable in that they actually speak in the present situation.

The relationship in life of the exegete to the subject determines the question or line of inquiry which the interpreter directs toward the text.[171] It is not enough merely to direct a question toward a text and seek an answer of something that happened in the past. Rather, to understand a text fully, one must seek to understand and feel what the original author felt and knew.[172]

The real aim of interpretation is to discover the possibility of human being revealed in a text.[173] The subjectivity of prior understanding is the only valid basis for attempting interpretation and understanding. Interpretation takes place only when the interpreter is touched in his own being by the text.[174] The prior understanding is not to be eliminated. Rather, it is to be brought into the consciousness and critically tested in one's understanding of the text.[175] Bultmann calls absurd the demand that the interpreter must silence his subjectivity in order to obtain objective knowledge. The result of interpretation is not thus foreordained. Rather, the direction of investigation is made possible.[176]

However one regards existential hermeneutics and demythologizing, Bultmann's intentions must be regarded as laudable. "It was precisely his concern for the communication of the gospel that led Rudolf Bultmann to his radical demythologizing of the New Testament."[177] In addition one can only appreciate Bultmann's concern for radical obedience to the ethical demands of God.[178] Also, a very definite concern for understanding one's presuppositions has been expressed by Bultmann,[179] although the use of Heiderggerian presupposition may raise questions for some biblical interpreters. However, some evaluations of his concepts need to be made.

The disjunction which Bultmann sees between the Old Testament and the New Testament actually proclaims New Testament religion as something new and different from Old Testament religion. The use of the Old Testament by early Christians, including Jesus himself, raises serious questions concerning the validity of such a sharp distinction between the Old and New Testaments as Bultmann makes.[180] Along with this disjunction Bultmann relegates the Old Testament to only a pedagogic function in Christianity. Further, he affirms that the Old Testament shares this function with other elements of Occidental history.[181] Although this is not Marcionism per se, the usefulness of the Old Testament for Christianity is effectively reduced to a minimum.

A part of Bultmann's separation of the Old Testament and New Testament is his view of the corporate nature of Old Testament religion. He affirms, however, that religion in the New Testament was no longer corporate but entirely individualistic.[182] Although Old Testament religion was certainly corporate, there was also an individual aspect.[183] Jeremiah and Ezekiel may have voiced the first definitive statement of individualism[184] but "individual leadership and responsibility, as well as personal religious experience, were recognized long before this."[185] Although the corporate structure of Israelite society was very strong, there was room also for individuality.[186] Neither was negated by the other. Further, religion as presented in the New Testament has some aspects of corporate structure. At least one major New Testament introduction finds the concept of community a necessary presupposition for understanding the New Testament.[187]

Bultmann has affirmed the necessity of presupposing the historical method of interrogating an ancient text. At the same time he makes abundantly clear that one does not hear the Word of God by using such procedure.[188] In other words, nothing must intervene between God and the individual--not the historical method nor even the ancient text. Thus, Bultmann seems to regard the historical method--and even the text--as unnecessary in the actual application of biblical concepts to individual lives. If the historical method is necessary, it assumes a minor role in the existential encounter with God.

The twofold emphasis which is called here historical interpretation and theological interpretation is quite apparent in the modern period. Historical interpretation has become a necessary part of biblical interpretation. At the same time there is a definite attempt by some scholars to go beyond historical interpretation. But in doing so there is a serious danger of destroying many of the gains realized by historical interpretation or of obscuring historical interpretation altogether. Typological interpretation tends to read the New Testament back into the Old Testament. Sensus plenior opens the Pandora's box of subjectivity in interpretation. Bultmann's existentialism is strongly Marcionist in tendency. Thus, all three methods tend to eliminate the importance of the Old Testament for Christianity. All three methods tend to look for a meaning in Scripture that is not on the surface, that is, a hidden meaning. As with allegorical interpretation there is the tendency to affirm the meaning discovered by these three methods of theological interpretation as the real meaning of Scripture. Thus, historical interpretation and theological interpretation begin to merge and the distinctions between them are obscured. Further, all three methods use techniques and criteria that go beyond or are other than the techniques of historical interpretation and the results of historical interpretation tend to be obscured. If historical interpretation is valid, the process and results of that interpretation must not be obliterated. Further, the results of historical interpretation must be the foundation of the process of application.[189]

¹Cf. Hahn, OTMR, pp. 1-43, 226-32.

²Above, pp. 4-5, 10-11.

³Hahn, OTMR, discusses several of these emphases. See also Carl. E. Braaten, History and Hermeneutics, Vol. II of New Directions in Theology, ed. by William Hordern (Philadelphia: Westminster Press, 1966).

⁴Tasker, The Old Testament in the New, pp. 10-11.

⁵Cf. Grobel, "Biblical Criticism," pp. 407-13; Grobel, "Interpretation, History and Principles of," pp. 718-24; De Vries, "Biblical Criticism, History of," pp. 413-18; R. M. Grant, The Bible in the Church, pp. 118-41.

⁶Hahn, OTMR, pp. 1-2.

⁷Smart, Interpretation, pp. 37-38.

⁸R. M. Grant, The Bible in the Church, p. 168, cf. p. 6.

⁹James Barr, Old and New in Interpretation, A Study of the Two Testaments (London: SCM Press, Ltd., 1966), p. 188.

¹⁰Hahn, OTMR, p. 41.

¹¹Grobel, "Biblical Criticism," p. 408. Cf. Hahn, OTMR, p. 2.

¹²Hahn, OTMR, p. 2.

¹³Grobel, "Biblical Criticism," pp. 412-13.

¹⁴Markus Barth, Conversation with the Bible, pp. 239-52.

¹⁵Cf. Wright, "Modern Issues in Biblical Studies: History and the Patriarchs," Expository Times, LXXI (July, 1960), 292.

[16] Cf. Hahn, *OTMR*, pp. 185-225.

[17] See above, Chapter I.

[18] Lampe and Woollcombe, *Essays on Typology*, p. 17.

[19] Smart, *Interpretation*, pp. 232-33. "History is particularly valuable in combating naive false assumptions. The theological student who is introduced to historical criticism in college or seminary comes frequently from a church where the use of Scripture has been completely uncritical, so that to him the approach is new and modern. He thinks of it simply as the intelligent approach in contrast to the unintelligent one. Therefore, he may develop a somewhat arrogant pride in what is no more than a smattering of superficial historical information that leaves him without any real grasp of the meaning of Scripture as a revelation of God to man today, and he may scorn the 'ignorant literalist' who unknown to him has been more open in his Bible reading to a word of judgment and promise from God than he himself. An introduction to the positive and negative achievements of historical criticism would dissipate his pride and make him aware of the sobering complexity of the problem in which he and his church are involved."

[20] Hahn, *OTMR*, p. 22.

[21] *Ibid.*, pp. 42-43.

[22] Michalson, "Bultmann against Marcion," *OTCF*, p. 49.

[23] Lampe and Woollcombe, *Essays on Typology*, pp. 14-17.

[24] Robert C. Dentan, "Typology--Its Use and

Abuse," *Anglican Theological Review*, XXXIV (October, 1952), 215.

²⁵ This is related to the statement above, p. 71, n. 2.

²⁶ Henry J. Cadbury, "The Peril of Archaizing Ourselves," *Interpretation*, III (July, 1949), 332.

²⁷ Smart, *Interpretation*, p. 133, says, "What is needed . . . in interpretation . . . is . . . a faithful exegesis and exposition of Scripture that will wrestle with the words of these ancient witnesses until the walls of the centuries become thin and they tell us in our day what they knew so well in their day" (underlining his).

²⁸ Cadbury, "The Peril of Archaizing Ourselves," p. 337, quoting Charles R. Joy in the introduction to Schweitzer's *Pyschiatric Study of Jesus* (Boston: The Beacon Press), 1948, p. 25, states,
"It is conceivable that religious truth might be preached independently of any age, truth that is universally and everlastingly so, truth that is valid for every succeeding generation and century. The simple fact, however, is that the truth that Jesus taught is not of that kind. He had a gospel of love to teach and then he wrapped it up in the ideas of his contemporaries. We cannot appropriate to ourselves this gospel of love by refusing to recognize the wrapping. Each age must unwrap the gospel and then apply it afresh to itself, which means, in all probability, enveloping it again."

²⁹ Wright, "The Problem of Archaizing Ourselves," p. 450.

³⁰ *Ibid.*, p. 451.
"There is absolutely no way by which we can rid ourselves of the problem of

archaism or assume that the past is past
and of no significance for the present.
Life involves a constant attempt to adjust ourselves to new situations in the
light of past experience. . . . Even
when we are fully aware of the dangers of
archaism, we still cannot rest content
with a static conception of the past in
relation to the future. To do so would be
to assume that the achievement of human
civilization in the past eight thousand
years was meaningless as far as the future is concerned."

[31] Wright, "Old Testament Scholarship in Prospect," p. 185.

[32] Wright, "Modern Issues," pp. 292-93. The historical framework of the patriarchal narratives has recently been questioned from another point of view. John Van Seters, "The Problem of Childlessness in Near Eastern Law and the Patriarchs of Israel," Journal of Biblical Literature, LXXXVII (December, 1968), 401-8.

[33] James Barr, "Revelation Through History in the Old Testament and in Modern Theology," Interpretation, XVII (April, 1963), 193-205. The same article appears in Martin E. Marty and Dean F. Peerman, eds., New Theology No. 1 (New York: The Macmillan Company, 1964), pp. 60-74. Cf. Von Rad, Old Testament Theology, II, 416, where he mentions this controversy.

[34] Barr, "Revelation Through History in the Old Testament and in Modern Theology," New Theology No. 1, p. 61.

[35] Ibid., p. 70.

[36] Smart, Interpretation, p. 172.

[37] Wright
"overstates his case by isolating the revelation in the event, so that he equates

history with revelation. . . . This tendency to equate revelation with the historical events fails to take account of the fact that, everywhere in Scripture, the revelation, which is the inmost meaning of the event, is hidden until it is revealed by the Spirit of God to the faith of man. The event itself is capable of receiving other interpretation." (Ibid., p. 173)

[38] The element of direct verbal communication between God and man is similar to an existential understanding of man's relation to God.

[39] See above, pp. 10-11.

[40] James D. Smart, "The Death and Rebirth of Old Testament Theology," Journal of Religion, XXIII, No. 1 (1943), 1-11; XXIII, No. 2 (1943), 125-36. Cf. Smart, Interpretation, Chapters 8 and 9, which present the same subject.

[41] Smart, "The Death and Rebirth of Old Testament Theology," No. 1, p. 3.

[42] Ibid.

[43] Ibid., p. 4

[44] Ibid.

[45] Muilenberg, "Preface to Hermeneutics," pp. 19-22.

[46] Ibid., p. 19.

[47] Horace D. Hummel, "Survey of Recent Literature," OTMR, p. 308.

[48] Ibid.

[49] Markus Barth, "The Old Testament in Hebrews," Current Issues in New Testament Interpretation, ed. by William Klassen and Graydon F. Snyder (New York;

Harper & Row, Publishers, 1962), p. 53.

[50]Floyd V. Filson, "Unity of the Old and the New Testament," Interpretation, V (April, 1951), 138-50.

[51]Carl E. Braaten, History and Hermeneutics, pp. 116-29.

[52]For a significant bibliography on typology see H. H. Rowley, The Unity of the Bible, p. 19n. See also Bright, Authority, p. 192n.

[53]See above, p. 48n17.

[54]Lampe and Woollcombe, Essays on Typology, p. 18; cf. Smart, Interpretation, p. 93.

[55]Smart, Interpretation, pp. 94-96.

[56]Ibid., p. 94.

[57]Gerhard von Rad, "Typological Interpretation of the Old Testament," Essays, p. 37.

[58]The debate is presented in Essays by Gerhard von Rad, "Typological Interpretation of the Old Testament," pp. 17-39; Martin Noth, "The 're-presentation' of the Old Testament in Proclamation," pp. 76-88; Friedrich Baumgartel, "The Hermeneutical problem of the Old Testament," pp. 134-59; Johann Jakob Stamm, "Jesus Christ and the Old Testament," pp. 200-210; Th. C. Vriezen, "Theocracy and Soteriology," pp. 211-23; Franz Hesse, "The Evaluation and the Authority of Old Testament Texts," pp. 285-313.

[59]Stamm, "Jesus Christ and the Old Testament," p. 202; cf. Vriezen, "Theocracy and Soteriology."

[60]Baumgartel, "The Hermeneutical Problem of the Old Testament," pp. 147-148.

[61]Ibid., p. 148.

[62] Ibid., p. 135.

[63] Von Rad, "Typological Interpretation," p. 19.

[64] Ibid., p. 17.

[65] Noth, "Re-presentation," p. 81.

[66] Ibid., p. 85.

[67] Lampe and Woollcombe, Essays on Typology, p. 9.

[68] Ibid., p. 11.

[69] Ibid., p. 10.

[70] Gerhard von Rad, "Typological Interpretation of the Old Testament," Essays, p. 22.

[71] J. R. Darbyshire, "Typology," Encyclopedia of Religion and Ethics, ed. by James Hastings, 1922, XII, 502-503.

[72] R. A. Markus, "Presuppositions of the Typological Approach to Scripture," Church Quarterly Review, CLVIII (October-December, 1957), 446-48.

[73] Cf. above, pp. 41-42.

[74] Dentan, "Typology--Its Use and Abuse," p. 212.

[75] Lampe and Woollcombe, Essays in Typology, p. 40.

[76] Ibid., p. 39.

[77] Ibid., p. 41.

[78] Ibid., pp. 39-40.

[79] Ibid., p. 40.

[80] Ibid., p. 29.

[81] Von Rad, "Typological Interpretation of the Old Testament," pp. 36-37.

[82] Ibid., p. 38. Von Rad's views are presented more fully in his Old Testament Theology, II, 317-429. See especially pp. 363-87.

[83] Von Rad, "Typological Interpretation of the Old Testament," p. 20. Cf. Hans Walter Wolff, "The Hermeneutics of the Old Testament," Essays, p. 180, where he also indicates a preference for the term "analogy." Smart also speaks of correspondences in Interpretation, p. 102. Smart entitles Chapter IV "Typology, Allegory, and Analogy."

[84] Markus, "Presuppositions of the Typological Approach to Scripture," p. 442.

[85] Lampe and Woollcombe, Essays in Typology, p. 29.

[86] Wolff, "The Hermeneutics of the Old Testament," pp. 181-82.

[87] Smart, Interpretation, pp. 115-16. Cf. p. 93.

[88] Wright, God Who Acts, p. 65.

[89] Ibid., p. 66.

[90] Wolff, "The Hermeneutics of the Old Testament," p. 184.

[91] Ibid., p. 185.

[92] Ibid., p. 191.

[93] Ibid., p. 183.

[94] Ibid., p. 182.

[95] Ibid., pp. 186-99.

[96] Cf. Bright, Authority, pp. 84-85.

[97] Raymond E. Brown, *The Sensus Plenior of Sacred Scripture* (Baltimore, Md.: St Mary's University, 1955). (Hereinafter referred to as *Sensus Plenior*.)

[98] *Ibid*., pp. 88-90.

[99] *Ibid*., p. 4. "The literal sense is that which both the Holy Spirit and the human author directly and proximately intended, and which the words directly convey, either properly or metaphorically."

[100] *Ibid*., p. 5.

[101] *Ibid*., p. 10. According to Brown a thing may be persons, actions, events, laws, and so forth.

[102] *Ibid*., p. 92.

[103] By "all scholars" Brown apparently means Catholic scholars.

[104] Brown, *Sensus Plenior*, p. 92.

[105] *Ibid*., p. 93

[106] *Ibid*., pp. 94-95.

[107] *Ibid*., p. 98.

[108] *Ibid*., p. 103.

[109] *Ibid*., pp. 100-101.

[110] *Ibid*., p. 102.

[111] *Ibid*., p. 105.

[112] *Ibid*., p. 113.

[113] *Ibid*., p. 127.

[114] *Ibid*., p. 119. Brown, p. 123, outlines the relationship of the literal and typical senses

in the following manner (underlining his):
"I. A division on the basis of the <u>Hagiographer's Knowledge</u>.
  "1. Clear understanding--The Literal Sense.
  "2. Lack of clear understanding--The Spiritual Sense:
    "a. Flowing from the text--The Sensus Plenior.
    "b. Flowing from 'things' described in the text--The Typical Sense.
"II. A Division on the basis of the <u>Material Object</u>.
  "1. Sense of words: ('Literal' in a very broad sense)
    "a. With <u>clear</u> knowledge by the hagiographer--The Literal Sense.
    "b. Without <u>clear</u> knowledge by the hagiographer--The Sensus Plenior."

[115] <u>Ibid.</u>, p. 122.

[116] <u>Ibid.</u>, p. 123.

[117] <u>Ibid.</u>, p. 124.

[118] <u>Ibid.</u>, p. 125.

[119] <u>Ibid.</u>, p. 126.

[120] <u>Ibid.</u>, p. 129.

[121] <u>Ibid.</u>, p. 130.

[122] <u>Ibid.</u>, p. 134.

[123] <u>Ibid.</u>

[124] <u>Ibid.</u>, p. 136.

[125] <u>Ibid.</u>, pp. 137-38.

[126] <u>Ibid.</u>, p. 145 (underlining his).

[127] <u>Ibid.</u>, p. 146.

[128] Ibid., p. 126.

[129] Ibid., p. 113.

[130] See the definition of sensus plenior above. Cf. Brown, Sensus Plenior, pp. 92-93.

[131] Ibid., pp. 94-95.

[132] Ibid., pp. 123-24.

[133] See below, Chapter IV, the discussion of continuing revelation and the unity of the Testaments.

[134] Rudolf Bultmann, "The Significance of the Old Testament for the Christian Faith," OTCF, p. 21; underlining his.

[135] Ibid., pp. 22-23.

[136] Ibid., p. 27.

[137] Ibid., p. 29.

[138] Rudolf Bultmann, "Prophecy and Fulfillment," Essays, p. 51

[139] Ibid., p. 55

[140] Ibid., p. 72.

[141] Ibid., p. 73

[142] Ibid.

[143] Ibid., p. 75.

[144] Ibid., p. 58.

[145] Ibid.

[146] Ibid., p. 73.

[147] Bultmann, "The Significance of the Old

Testament for the Christian Faith," p. 11.

¹⁴⁸Ibid., p. 21.

¹⁴⁹Ibid., pp. 13-14.

¹⁵⁰Ibid., p. 20.

¹⁵¹Ibid., p. 21.

¹⁵²Ibid., p. 17.

¹⁵³Ibid., p. 16.

¹⁵⁴Ibid., p. 17.

¹⁵⁵See above p. 87n134.

¹⁵⁶Bultmann, "The Significance of the Old Testament for the Christian Faith," p. 21.

¹⁵⁷Ibid., p. 23.

¹⁵⁸Ibid., p. 27.

¹⁵⁹Ibid., p. 29.

¹⁶⁰Ibid., p. 30; underlining his.

¹⁶¹Ibid., p. 32.

¹⁶²Bright, Authority, p. 69.

¹⁶³Bultmann, "The Significance of the Old Testament for the Christian Faith," p. 34.

¹⁶⁴Ibid., p. 35.

¹⁶⁵For the present purpose two articles are of special significance. Rudolf Bultmann, "The Problem of Hermeneutics," Essays--Philosophical and Theological, trans. by James C. G. Creig (London: SCM Press, Ltd., 1955), pp. 234-61, and Rudolf Bultmann, "Is Exegesis without Presuppositions Possible?" Existence and Faith, trans. by Schubert

M. Ogden (New York: Meridian Books, Inc., 1960), pp. 289-96.

[166] Bultmann, "Is Exegesis without Presuppositions Possible?" pp. 289-90.

[167] Ibid., p. 291.

[168] Ibid.

[169] Ibid., p. 292.

[170] Ibid., p. 294; underlining his.

[171] Bultmann, "The Problem of Hermeneutics," p. 243.

[172] Ibid., p. 246.

[173] Ibid., pp. 250-51.

[174] Ibid., p. 256.

[175] Ibid., pp. 253-54.

[176] Ibid., pp. 255-56.

[177] Bright, Authority, p. 177.

[178] Rudolf Bultmann, Theology of the New Testament, Vol. I (New York: Charles Scribner's Sons, 1959), pp. 11-15.

[179] Above, pp. 92-93.

[180] See below, the discussion of the unity of the Testaments, Chapter IV.

[181] Bultmann, "The Significance of the Old Testament for the Christian Faith," p. 31.

[182] See above, pp. 90-91. Cf. Bultmann, "The Significance of the Old Testament for the Christian Faith,: pp. 21-30.

[183] Eichrodt, *Theology of the Old Testament*, II, 231-32, stresses the interplay rather than opposition of these two aspects.

[184] Jer. 31:29; Ezek. 18:4, 20; cf. Deut. 24:16.

[185] J. W. Flight, "Man and Society," *IDB*, III, 250.

[186] Eichrodt, *Theology of the Old Testament*, II, 239.

[187] Howard Clark Kee, Franklin W. Young, and Karlfried Froelich, *Understanding the New Testament* (2nd ed.; Englewood Cliffs, N. J.: Prentice-Hall, Inc., 1965), P. viii.

[188] Bultmann, "The Significance of the Old Testament for the Christian Faith," pp. 21, 30.

[189] Typology and *sensus plenior* as presented above specifically insist that historical interpretation is the foundation for theological interpretation.

CHAPTER IV

A PROPOSED SOLUTION TO THE PROBLEM OF THE

RELEVANCE OF THE OLD TESTAMENT

FOR THE CHRISTIAN FAITH

## The need to Separate Exegesis and application

The solution proposed here can be summarized in three statements corresponding to three major steps in the hermeneutical process. The first step is historical interpretation or exegesis. The second step is the derivation of principles of relationship with God. The third step is theological interpretation, or application. However, before these three steps are discussed in detail some preliminary matters need to be presented.

The study of representative methods of interpretation indicates the need to separate explicitly historical hermeneutics and theological hermeneutics, that is, to separate exegesis and application, although they are bound together in the person who applies the Old Testament to modern society.[1] Historical hermeneutics and theological hermeneutics need to be separated in order to clarify terminology. The determination of the religion of the Old Testament is sometimes stated to be a very vital part of the work of the biblical specialist[2] and the term "theology" is used to describe this element of interpretation.[3] Since the task of finding meaning for modern man also is called theology (theological interpretation or biblical theology) it becomes vital to an understanding of the Bible to specify precisely what one is doing. Historical interpretation and theological interpretation are two different things although vitally related.

The separation of exegesis and application

is also necessary in order to see clearly that both are needed. There is still antagonism and lack of understanding among those who advocate one approach above the other.[4] An examination of the methods advocated by those who stress historical hermeneutics reveals that they often slide almost intuitively from exegesis to application or do not sufficiently clarify the process of application.[5] On the other hand, those who most strongly advocate a theological approach to the Bible are often accused of imposing their own biases upon the Bible.[6] In either case, however, scholars usually insist that historical interpretation is necessary and that biblical interpretation involves more than the historical element.[7]

Clear and distinct separation of historical hermeneutics from theological hermeneutics is necessary in order to prevent the overemphasis of either approach. The current emphasis on biblical theology stemmed from a desire to reduce and overcome the previous overemphasis of historical pursuits. The excessive emphasis of historical interpretation as epitomized by Wellhausenism had stagnated and prevented necessary theological and spiritual insights. But Craig has firmly stated that

> the present revolt is in grave danger of becoming a retreat to dogma rather than an advance to a truer insight into the permanent significance of the events recorded in the Old and New Testaments. That peril can be met only as men of sound historical training accept the challenge to interpret the meaning of Christian faith.[8]

Thus, overemphasis of theological interpretation must also be avoided.

A further indication of the need to separate exegesis from application is the consideration of one or many meanings for Scripture.[9] The need to apply the Old Testament to many different situations seems to call for the possibility of multiple interpretations. However, this diametrically opposes a primary emphasis of historical interpretation that only one meaning is possible when the historical milieu is adequately reconstructed. The separation of exegesis from application makes possible a proper insistence upon one historical meaning for Scripture and yet makes possible also a new meaning each time the Old Testament is applied to a new situation. The new meaning is not a new historical meaning. The one historical meaning is appropriated in a new situation. In this sense application is really appropriation of the historical understanding of the biblical material.

Although historical interpretation and theological interpretation need to be separated, an either/or situation must not be permitted. They must operate alongside each other in the field of biblical science and ultimately they must operate together within the individual interpreter. Rylaarsdam's discussion of the two possible ways of reading the Bible is significant at this point.[10] One is related to historical interpretation and the other to theological interpretation. The great gulf that is often apparent between scholars and preachers illustrates the necessity for both to operate together.[11] The goal, however, is not that the scholar should at times come down to earth nor that the preacher should exhibit flashes of scholarship before his congreagation. "The real goal is an awareness of a common task, an awareness that preacher and biblical scholar alike deal with the word of God and are to be involved in the exposition of Scripture."[12] The necessity for such an awareness is discussed by Smart in terms of exegesis and exposition.[13] Smart takes Vriezen to task for assuming that exegesis and exposition can operate largely in separation from each other with the preacher combining the two. Certainly preaching is dependent upon sound historical interpretation, as Smart affirms. However, Smart goes further and insists that exegesis is also inseparable from exposition.[14]

In utilizing both historical and theological hermeneutics at the same time, care must be taken so they are not confused. Confusion results when the claim is made that theological hermeneutics is something different than historical hermeneutics but is at the same time a part of the critical approach. Thus, the difference between historical hermeneutics and theological hermeneutics tends to be obliterated and the real nature of theological interpretation as application is obscured. Therefore, there is a need to separate historical hermeneutics from theological hermeneutics and explicitly define the latter.

## Assumptions Underlying a Solution

In additon to considering the separation of exegesis and application, some assumptions underlying the solution proposed below also need to be considered. First, it is assumed that the <u>Old Testament</u> will be made applicable to Christain life. That is, the Old Testament must remain the Old Testament. The method of interpretation must not make it a New Testament pre-written or impose the Old Testament upon the New Testament. In some instances, the difference between the Testaments is so emphasized that the Old Testament virtually has no standing of its own as a message for Christians today.[15] In other instances, the unity of the Testaments is emphasized to an extreme.[16] Inescapably the question of the unity of the Testaments must be considered.[17]

Discontinuity is often found in two factors. If the historical nature of the Old Testament is taken seriously, then there is much that is time conditioned in the Old Testament and therefore of little value for the Christian.[18] Also, discontinuity is seen in what is considered the radical nature of the Christ-event. In other words, New Testament religion is regarded as different than Old Testament religion. For instance, Bright states, "We have admitted--for it is not be denied-- that the faith of the Old Testament is not indentical with the Christian faith."[19] On the other hand, it is recognized that Jesus himself used the Old Testament as Scripture.[20] However, Mickelsen suggests that the diversity between the Testaments may play just as great a role in God's purpose as unity.[21] "God not only controls the diversity, but he uses it to clarify the meaning of life and His relationship to man."[22] Certainly the discontinuity between the Testaments should not be overemphasized.

The unity of the Bible is usually seen in one or more of several factors. Usually it is affirmed that the same God who revealed himself in the Old Testament period is also the God of the New Testament.[23] If the same God revealed himself in both Testaments, it is reasonable to assume that many of the concepts will be the same in both Testaments. The doctrine of sin, for instance, appears in the New Testament, as it does in the Old, as rebellion against God and with the individual sinner responsible for his own sin.[24] The result of sin is seen as death or separation from God in both Testaments. Salvation by faith is as much a part of the Old Testament religion as it is of New Testament religion.[25] The kingdom of God and the suffering servant are also found in both Testaments.

Unity is also found in the idea of fulfillment. Rowley suggests that fulfillment can be seen in patterns observable in both Testaments-- in the law, in the idea of the suffering servant, in the covenant.[26] Bright affirms that fulfillment gives a unity to the Testaments because "the redemptive purposes of God, begun in Abraham and the Exodus, have come to fulfillment in Jesus Christ--and this is the whole meaning of God's history with his people, maybe, of history altogether."[27]

Unity is also recognized because of the historical continuity of the community of Israel and the Church. That is, the Church is a direct outgrowth of the Israel of the Old Testament. This reflected in the self-understanding of Jesus. He used the Scriptures, that is, the Old Testament, and indicated that he was the fulfillment of the promises made there. Similar to this is the view of Freedman that "the historical continuity of the community of Israel and its conviction concerning a continuing, active relationship with the one living God"[28] is the basis for unity. A genetic relationship between the Testaments is suggested by Rowley when he states that the seeds of monotheism, ethical religion, and covenant found in Moses reveals a unity in diversity.[29]

The unity of the Bible is further demonstrated by Paul's discussion of the relationship of the Jew and the Gentile in Ephesians, chapters 2 and 3. In 2:11-22, he develops the idea of the union of the Jew and Gentile in the church.[30] Both Jews and Gentiles who believe in Christ have become members of the household of God. This implies that the Jews had strayed from the household of God. Nevertheless, it is the household of God which stands as the unifying factor, that is, relationship with God. God intended this relationship in the Old Testament. When the Jews strayed, he renewed the relationship through Christ as described in the New Testament.

Some scholars seem to lean to the view of discontinuity of the Testaments even while affirming the unity. Freedman feels that the nature of Israel's relationship with God is so inadequately understood that one should probably not expect to find a general pattern under which all of the Bible can be subsumed.[31] Similarly, Bright, while affirming the existence of a structure of faith in the Old Testament and througout the Bible, nevertheless says that "no single set question can possibly do justice to every text. . . . We must let each text pose its own questions, whatever these may be.[32]

Perhaps the best answer to the question of the unity of the Testaments is that given by the Church in the second century and in succeeding centuries. The unity of the Testaments could not be tangibly demonstrated. In fact, Marcion had demonstrated some elements of discontinuity. Nevertheless, the Church affirmed by faith that the Old Testament was a part of Christian Scripture

and belonged in the Bible. Essentially, this is
the answer to the question of unity in the twentieth century. The unity of the Testaments involves
a confessional statement grounded in a faith commitment on the part of a believing people.[33]

The position taken here is that the same
God who revealed himself in the Old Testament also
revealed himself in the New Testament and is revealing himself to men today. Also, this writer
feels that the religion of the Old Testament is
basically the same as the religion of the New Testament. Rowley states that the religion found in the
Testaments is "man's response to the achieved work
of God, his yielding to the constraint of grace, his
fellowship with God and obedience to Him, his reflection of the Spirit of God in every aspect of
his life, and the lifting of his life into the purpose of God."[34] However, one must do more than
simply affirm the unity of the Testaments. Some
consideration must be given to the elements of
discontinuity and to the way in which these are
affected by the unifying elements. The differences
between the Testaments are either in God, in the
revelation of God, or in men as they apprehend
the revelation. If the same God revealed himself
in both Testaments, then this is certainly not an
element of discontinuity. To some persons there
may be a question about the revelation of God. Did
God reveal himself as fully in the Old Testament
period as he did in the New Testament period through
Jesus? Jesus' discussion of divorce in Matthew 19
indicates that the revelation of the Old Testament
was quite adequate. Further, Jesus pointed out
that the deficiency of understanding was due to the
lack of apprehension on the part of the Hebrew people
rather than some failure or lack on the part of God
or the revelation of himself to the people. This
brings the discussion to the way in which men
apprehended the revelation of God. The difference
between the Testaments apparently lies in the apprehension of the revelation of God and in the way in
which it was expressed.[35] That is, as men apprehended the revelation of God, they expressed their
understanding of God by means of the idiom of their

own culture. It is these cultural elements in the Old Testament and in the New which are no longer binding upon twentieth-century Christians. However, God did reveal himself to the people in biblical times. They did understand and apprehend the revelation to some degree. It is just this revelation of God which must be apprehended by twentieth-century Christians.

A second assumption is that revelation continues and is personal.[36] A prime consideration in the unity of the Testaments is that the same God who revealed himself to people in Old Testament times also revealed himself to people in New Testament times. Corollary to this is that the same God continues to reveal himself to people today. In revealing himself to people in the Old Testament period, God demanded from them loyalty and commitment to himself as expressed in their relationship to God and to other people. The same God made the same demands as he revealed himself to people in the New Testament period. Nothing less should be expected today. Thus, revelation is to people from whom is expected a personal response to God. In other words, revelation is personal.

H. Wheeler Robinson has a pertinent discussion of the personal quality of revelation. Although an external guarantor of the authority of revelation may be sought, usually the Bible or the Church, when pushed to its initiation, each is dependent upon a person who believed, was convicted, that revelation had taken place. In final analysis, none other than God himself is the guarantor and this is not in some kind of objective overwhelming experience but in personal relationship.[37]

The personal dimension of revelation can be seen from several directions. From a philosophical viewpoint, Polanyi affirms that all knowledge is personal.[38] Personal knowledge is a fusion of the personal and objective and requires a framework of commitment.[39] Even in the scientific realm

the act of knowing involves an appraisal of the
evidences. He decries the traditional dichotomy
of objective and subjective. The "personal co-
efficient, which shapes all factual knowledge,
bridges . . . the disjunction between subjectivity
and objectivity."[40] Although Polanyi denies that
such personal participation is subjective,[41] the
charge may have some validity.

    From the point of view of inspiration of
Scripture James Smart emphasizes the personal element. He contends that the inspiration of the
Bible is basically similar to Jesus' inspiration.[42]
Two extremes of viewpoint have emphasized the humanity of Jesus as against his divinity or vice
versa. These same viewpoints have also been applied to the Bible. In other words, inspiration
is dynamic, not static.[43] A person is inspired and
then produces written words.[44] Such was the major
emphasis in the Old Testament. The rabbinic
emphasis upon the law and a written record distorted this dynamic viewpoint. It appeared once
again in Jesus. "The movement of the Spirit of God
in Israel that brought the Old Testament into
being burst forth with new power in Jesus Christ
and his church."[45] The emphasis here is that a
person in a particular relationship with God is
moved by God, convicted, and out of this kind of
relationship produces a life that can be said to
be inspired. If a part of that life involves the
production of written words, they may be said to
be a revelation from God. That is, the ultimate
source of the words is God.

    In the same fashion, the authority of the
Bible stems from this kind of personal relationship
with God. Bernard Ramm states that most books on
religious authority affirm God as the final authority in religion.[46] Ramm also makes this affirmation and begins his discussion with the authority
of God. God expresses his authority by divine
self-revelation.[47]

> There is an __external__ principle (the in-
> spired Scripture) and an __internal__ principle

(the witness of the Holy Spirit). It is the principle of an objective <u>divine</u> revelation, with an interior <u>divine witness</u>. These two principles must always be held together, so that it may be said either that: (1) our authority is the Holy Spirit speaking in the Scriptures, or, (2) our authority is the Scriptures sealed to us by the Holy Spirit.[48]

In speaking of such personal dimensions one must beware of reducing God, or at least the revelation of God, to the internal psychical experience of the individual. To go in this direction is to permit any imagining of the mind to have the authority of an authentic revelation from God. Smart expresses a similar viewpoint in speaking of exegesis and exposition.[49] Although personal knowledge of God allows room for a large amount of subjectivity, the Bible, as the recorded experiences of others who had a personal knowledge of God, stands as an objective referent which can prevent excesses of subjectivity. The experiences of men in the past therefore become models for twentieth-century Christians.

The personal quality of revelation is important in interpreting the Bible because the Bible itself is revelation for Christians today.[50] When God revealed himself in the Old Testament period, he demanded personal response from those to whom revelation was given. Personal response was made on the basis of the revelation that the people apprehended. If it was apprehended incorrectly or inadequately, the response was either incorrect or inadequate. Today, if the biblical revelation is apprehended incorrectly or inadequately, the personal response to God may very well be incorrect or inadequate. Thus, definite guidelines for apprehending the biblical revelation are needed, that is, rules for interpreting the Bible are necessary.

Since revelation is personal, its application must be to persons. That is, if the Old

Testament is relevant, it is relevant for Christians who are seeking guidance in the concrete situations of their lives. Abstract religious principles or principles of conduct, even if derived from the Bible, will not adequately make the Old Testament relevant for Christians today. A method of interpreting the Old Testament will be adequate only if it enables Chrisitans to apply the religious principles to their lives.[51]

    Thus, there are not any universal religious principles, only principles that appear in tne lives of persons as they live by them. Any principles derived from the Old Testament must be inductively determined from the lives of people as they lived in relationship to God. In turn, these principles are valid only when they are applied to the lives of people today. Just as illustrations in sermons serve as windows whereby the listener can understand more clearly what the preacher is saying, the lives of Old Testament people in relationship to God serve as windows whereby twenieth-century people can see what relationship to God ought to be today.

    A further consideration in continuing revelation is the question of the canon. The question of the canon is raised for several reasons. Revelation in Old Testament times resulted ultimately in a canon regardless of the time at which the canon was regarded as closed. If revelation continues as it did in Old Testament times, then in theory it could still result in the production of canonical materials. Also, according to Stendahl, historical hermeneutics, raises the question of the canon in its sharpest form. Extra-canonical material, for example the intertestamental literature, may be as valuable or more valuable than canonical material for a descriptive approach. Beyond the descriptive approach, however, the canon of Scripture becomes crucial.[52] From this, two questions may be raised. Why is the canon closed and why is it regarded as authoritative for Christians?

In regard to the first question, the canon is closed, for all practical purposes, because it is sufficient. It provides sufficient information, when adequately interpreted, for the establishment of a personal relationship with God by the person who reads it. It provides sufficient instruction, when adequately interpreted, for the living of the Christian life. The canon is closed then, not by something inherent in the materials themselves, but as a consequence of the faith of the Church.

John Bright reasons that the canon is closed because Christ is the eschatological event promised in the Old Testament. Since witness is given to it in the New Testament and there can never be a primary witness to this event again, the canon must be closed.[53] The reasoning is that there is no witness to God's revelation subsequent to the New Testament which can add anything to that revelation.

The answer to the second question is also largely a matter of faith.[54] It is in the canon that Christians believe they have a trustworthy guide to the way in which ancient people applied their understanding of God to life. It is just this application of godly (divine) principles to life which is the example followed today. Out of this application principles may be derived which can make the Christian teachings applicable to modern life.

A third assumption is that any proposed method of interpretation must be one that can be used by non-technically trained persons. In short, the method must make the Old Testament available to the majority of Christians while still being a method that is usable by the scholar. There should not be one method of interpretation of the Old Testament for scholars and another method for non-technically trained persons.[55]

There are perhaps three areas of interest in biblical studies.[56] The research specialist primarily devotes his time and attention to

questions of historical biblical research. The
professional can be represented by the pastor of a
church who must make use of the specialist's find-
to lead his church to make present-tense decisions about religious matters. The layman, who
is neither a professional nor a research specialist must have enough knowledge of the historical
biblical materials to enable him to make reasonable present-tense decisions. However, the vast
majority of Christians in any age are not historical scholars nor professionals. If the Bible is
used at all, it is usually used without the bene-
fit of technical historical training or skills.
Therefore, in suggesting a method for determining
the relevance of the Old Testament, one must not
suggest a method that will automatically shut out
most Christians. However, this does not mean that
the layman has no need of a historical understanding of the Old Testament.[57]

If the one method of historical biblical
interpretation is going to be that which is normally used by the specialist, as most scholars would
affirm, then it must be clarified and simplified
for use by laymen. In addition, the principles of
theological hermeneutics must also be set forth
clearly.

## Solutions Proposed by Others

Before proceeding to clarify exegetical
principles and to set forth principles of theological interpretation, a study of methods proposed
by others will help give perspective both to the
problem of relevance and to the various considerations which must be a part of a satisfactory
solution. Several attempts have been made to
apply the Old Testament to the Christian life.[58]

The solution offered by Harvey H. Guthrie
is based upon a study of certain dominant themes
which he feels appear in the Psalms of the Old
Testament. His point with regard to the problem
of relevance is that Israel's psalms constitute a

paradigm of the problems presented by all of the biblical heritage.[59] Guthrie asserts that Israel adopted certain cultural idioms as a means of praising God but that the idioms were transformed by the content they were made to carry.[60] The content of the psalms, as affirmed by Guthrie, is apparently the sovereignty of Yahweh. Yahweh's sovereignty has meaning in relationship to the people of God who proclaimed that sovereignty. Thus, Guthrie speaks also of the "divine call, the promise, and the covenant commitment."[61]

Guthrie makes clear that in order for the Old Testament to be relevant one must begin with the historical context in which the Bible comes to us. "When Israel defined herself and the character of her God against the culture by which she was surrounded, she enunciated her mythos in language and idioms derived from that culture."[62] Only by understanding the historical context of the songs of Israel is it possible to determine and understand the theological content of the psalms. "The divine call, the promise, and the covenant commitment are not capable of extraction from that series of moments which are a share of our past."[63]

However, the author's intent is not to affirm the past, but rather, to affirm the present, to show how presentday language and cultural idioms can be used to carry the theological content of the psalms. Just at this point some confusion is apparent. He has affirmed that the theological content of the psalms cannot be extracted from "that series of moments which are its share of our past."[64] However, he does seem to advocate the extraction of the biblical message from its historical context. "Study of the psalms of Israel further makes it clear that proclamation of God's work is tied to no particular cultural idiom, to no specific theology, to no particular mythos."[65]

As with other scholars, Guthrie insists that the the process of interpretation must begin with historical considerations. Further, he demonstrates that the biblical message can be reinterpreted in each succeeding generation so that it is always relevant. But he does not indicate how such reinterpretation should be done in the twentieth century.

James Smart, in two companion volumes, presents his principles of interpretation and seven illustrations of his method.[66] His method he calls Christological.[67] The title of his second volume reveals the emphasis of his method. Dialogue is a two-way conversation which, when it involves a person reading the Bible, is really a conversation between the reader and God. "This dialogue character is intrinsic to the content of the Scripture and for that reason is essential to the interpretation of it."[68] The dialogue between God, who is revealed in the Bible, and the reader of the Bible is intended to bring the reader into fellowship with God, to make him know his blindness (sin) and at the same time to give him sight (salvation; life more abundant).

Two factors are apparent in this emphasis upon dialogue. One factor concerns itself with the unity of the Bible and the fact that God who revealed himself in biblical times continues to reveal himself today. Smart affirms that Israel in both Old Testament and New Testament times passed through changes in language and thought forms while maintaining a continuity of her dialogue with God. "The _form_ of the dialogue changes and takes on new aspects, but in _substance_ it remains the same dialogue."[69] In this continuing dialogue with God, each person is free to have fellowship with God, that is, to dialogue with God, in terms of his own language and culture.

The second factor in Smart's method is indicated by the term "dialogue" itself. He stresses that a personal relationship with God is necessary in interpretation. "Only where men have come awake to the dependence of their lives upon a relationship with God in which God Speaks and man responds and have recognized the continuity of that modern dialogue with the dialogue laid bare in the Scriptures have they the sine qua non of interpretation."[70] Further, in discussing the problem of human nature, Smart says, "The most basic and decisive aspect of man's life is his relation with God, and . . . he cannot know himself apart from this relation"[71]

In the first two illustrations of his method, Smart makes clear that twentieth-century man must read the Bible from the point of view of twentieth-century scientific mentality. Certain factors in the Old Testament material are therefore not binding upon the twentieth-century Christain because they belong to the time and culture of the first hearer or reader of the Old Testament. In discussing Genesis 1, he says, "The first thing we do is establish our right to hear it with twentieth-century ears, while at the same time we concede to the author the right to speak as the inhabitant of a pre-scientific age."[72] In the second illustration of his method, Smart discusses Genesis, chapters 2 and 3, and says, "The key obstacle in the way of fruitful dialogue between these chapters and modern man is that the ancient tradition has gathered influence from many mythological elements that are strange and perplexing to the mind in an unmythological age such as ours."[73]

In this interpretation he does not clarify what is permanently binding in the Old Testament. Apparently this is related to the second factor in his method, but he does not state his procedure specifically. Twentieth-century scientific mentality seems to carry more weight in his actual procedure than does the idea of relatiohship with God. Smart describes the method as he practices it in his classroom.[74] Before historically interpreting a biblical text, he asks his class to list the questions that might be raised by the text in the minds of modern readers. These are set aside and the historical task completed. The questions are examined then, one by one, after which the overall theme of the passage is stated along with secondary themes. These themes show the theology of the text. Finally,

the students are asked to state the points at which
contemporary times contradict the theology of the
passage.

Smart definitely insists upon thorough
historical interpretation. His discussion of the
dialogue nature of the biblical revelation makes
plain also his insistence that application must
be made to modern man. However, he does not
specifically indicate how he bridges the gap between historical interpretation and application.
He slides almost intuitively from exegesis to
application.

John Bright approaches the question of the
relevance of the Old Testament from the point of
view of the authority of the Old Testament. Does
the Old Testament have a legitimate place in the
canon of Christian Scripture, and, if so, "How
are these ancient laws, institutions, and concepts,
these ancient narratives, sayings, and expressions
of an ancient piety, actually to be taken as
authoritative over the faith and life of the
Christian, and how proclaimed as such in the
church?"[75] The Church is accustomed to affirm
that the Bible, all of it, including the Old
Testament, is the supreme authority for the Christian.[76] However, there are parts of the Old Testament which, Christians generally agree, are no
longer binding upon Christians--ceremonial laws
(yet the tithe, which is a ceremonial law, is
held to be binding upon Christians); civil regu-
lations; and things in the Old Testament which
offend Christian conscience. But on what basis
are some aspects of the Old Testament regarded as
no longer binding while others are regarded as
binding on Christians?

To solve this problem, Bright first of all
examines some of the "classical" solutions which
have been attempted. Some persons have rejected
the Old Testament in the manner of Marcion. All
those who would place the Old Testament on a
level of value secondary to the New Testament
(Bright here includes Bultmann) are Marcionist in
tendency, according to Bright. Others have sought

to retain the Old Testament by reading a Christian meaning into it. The early Church Fathers did this by means of allegory and typology. The christological emphasis of the Reformers was akin to allegory, according to Bright. More recent tendencies in this direction include the emphasis called <u>sensus plenior</u> and the emphasis of Karl Barth.[77] A third group have attempted to solve the problem by evaluating the Old Testament material on the basis of a norm taken from outside the Old Testament, usually from the New Testament. Such a norm was usually isolated by means of a subjective value judgment.[78] Bright feels that this method is still very much in evidence, especially among the rank and file in the churches.[79] Thus Bright sees the classical solutions as attempting to remove the Old Testament from the Bible in the way of Marcion or attempting to save the Old Testament for Christianity by finding Christian meaning in its texts or by means of a normative principle derived from the New Testament.[80]

Against these attempts either to reject the Old Testament or to evaluate it by using a basis from outside the Old Testament, Bright strongly affirms that the Old Testament must be taken in its plain sense and that sense must be exegetically derived.[81] The plain meaning of the Old Testament must be folowed "through history to see how it was taken up in the New Testament, and then, from that perspective, we may look back and again understand the Old."[82] As this proposal is worked out in detail, it will reveal that "the key to the solution of the problem is to be found in the theological structure of both Testaments in their mutual relationships," that is, in the theological structure which binds the Testaments together.[83] Bright is here talking about biblical theology which he describes as historical and descriptive.[84] "We must press on behind the various different witnesses to lay hold of the structure of belief that underlies and informs them, and of which they are all in one way or another expressions."[85] According to Bright, this structure of theology is God's purposive activity, God's action in history. The

Old Testament, according to Bright, offers a theological interpretation of history.[86] Election, covenant, and promise are some of the significant elements in this Old Testament structure of theology. It is this promise which Bright believes is taken up in the New Testament and is fulfilled.[87] "Indeed, one can go so far as to say that the structure of the New Testament's theology is essentially the same as that of the Old, but with the content radically transformed in the light of what Christ has done."[88]

In applying this understanding to the problem as set forth in his initial discussion, Bright issues a plea for a return to biblical preaching--preaching which begins with exegesis, attempts to determine the theology of the text, and therefore is able to speak to twentieth-century man.[89] "It is . . . precisely through its theology that the biblical word to the then and there of an ancient age speaks to us in the here and now."[90] Finally, the word of the text must be translated into the idiom of today.

In summary, it can be seen that Bright also insists that historical interpretation must be done first. He is also very explicit that the Old Testament is relevant to the Christian faith. In fact, this is the point of his whole book. But he does not say precisely how the Old Testament is to be made relevant. He seems to slide almost intuitively from exegesis to application, a thing of which he has accused Vischer with the understanding that this is an incorrect procedure.[91] Further, Bright insists that no precise hermeneutical principle is possible.[92] "No single set question can possibly do justice to every text. . . . We must let each text pose its own questions, whatever these may be."[93] However, his suggestion that the Old Testament speaks to twentieth-century man through its theology is suggestive and perhaps related to the idea of deriving principles from the Old Testament.[94]

In actual practice, Bright makes the Old

Testament merely pedagogic.[95] Although Bright has emphatically stated that the Old Testament should not be limited only to this purpose, he affirms that as the Old Testament causes men to see themselves in B.C. perspective, "it addresses us and begins to serve its proper function as a preparation for the gospel."[96]

Related to this is his affirmation of the radical discontinuity of the Old Testament and New Testament religion. Although Bright very pointedly asserts that the Old Testament must not only be retained in the canon but must have relevancy for the Christian,[97] he nevertheless can say that "the Old Testament religion is indeed not identical with Christianity."[98] He can say that the content of Old Testament theology has been radically transformed by what Christ has done.[99] He can say that Old Testament religion is genetically related to Christianity but is not the same.[100] Despite his retention of the Old Testament in the canon and his insistence that it is relevant for the Christian faith, in practice he relegates the Old Testament to a position of lesser importance. Because of the discontinuity he sees between Old Testament and New Testament religion Bright insists that the Old Testament message must be preached "from an A.D. perspective, in its Christian significance."[101]

All the suggested solutions examined above have definite similarities. Each insists that interpretation must begin with historical interpretation, that is, exegesis. Each attempts to show that the biblical material not only can be applied but must be applied to modern man. Each is somewhat vague as to specific procedures for moving from exegesis to application. They move almost intuitively through this part of the process of interpretation. By starting with historical interpretation each of these suggested solutions affirms that there are differences between the Old Testament and the New Testament. By moving on to application they affirm that there is also unity between the Testaments and, furthermore, unity between the Testaments and the twentieth century. However, at the point of the unity of the Testaments, there is a significant difference between these suggested solutions. The difference between them can be illustrated in the form of a brief chart.

> Guthrie--cultural idiom (different)--content--(same)[102]
>
> Smart--form (different)--content (same)[103]
>
> Bright--structure (same)--substance (different)[104]

Guthrie and Smart apparently believe that the religion (content) of the Testaments is the same even though it is expressed in different cultural idioms. Bright's viewpoint seems to be diametrically opposed to the emphasis of Guthrie and Smart. One reviewer of Bright's The Authority of the Old Testament has raised this very question.

> (According to Bright,) the NT is radically different from the OT because, while "the structure of the NT's theology is essentially the same as that of the OT," the content is "radically transformed in the light of what Christ has done." But if the unifying "structure of belief" is a theology, then to change its content is surely to change its structure, i.e., is simply to change it. What then constitutes the continuity?[105]

However, Smart's method is very similar in one respect to that proposed by Bright. Each insists that the determination of the theology of a text will reveal what is permanently binding and commands the attention of men of every age.[106]

An examination of the solutions proposed by Guthrie, Smart, and Bright further indicates the necessity of starting with historical interpretation. In addition, the results of historical interpretation must be used in some way to make a valid application. The vagueness with which the above three viewpoints move from exegesis to application indicates the need for a precise statement of this part of the process.

## Clarification of Exegetical Principles

As stated above, there are three steps in the process of interpretation: historical interpretation (exegesis), reducing the Scripture to principles, and theological interpretation (application). Each step must be adequately clarified and simplified so that non-technically trained persons can use the process without destroying its validity for technically trained persons. In the clarification of exegetical principles, it will be helpful to examine some representative statements of these principles.

A. Berkely Mickelsen divides hermeneutical principles into two basic areas: general hermeneutics and special hermeneutics.[107] Under general hermeneutics he discusses context, language, history, and culture. Under special hermeneutics, he discusses short figures of speech, extended figures of speech, typology, symbols and symbolic actions, prophecy, descriptive language of creation and climax, poverty, doctrinal teachings, devotion, and conduct.

By context he means the immediate biblical context of a passage and the ideas in the biblical material.[108] Thus, context is a study of the Bible itself. Language is, of course, a study of the biblical language and the meanings involved. The third area under his terminology general hermeneutics is history and culture. The elements which he discusses under this heading are geographical factors, political factors, environmental factors of every-day living such as material culture, social-religious situation, and stability of economy. From his discussion it is clear that he is talking about the total cultural situation in which the original writer or hearers of the biblical message found themselves. Thus, under general hermeneutics, he has basically two areas--biblical study and a wider cultural study which will throw light upon various ideas and words in the biblical material.

Mickelsen divides his discussion of special hermeneutics into special literary forms and specific topical areas.[109] The special literary forms are elements of language. The specific topical areas include doctrinal teachings and devotion and conduct. Doctrinal teaching is really an illustrative explanation of the way in which the principles he has already enunciated should be used.[110] By devotional conduct he refers to a personal application of the biblical material to one's life. significantly, he says,

> Personal application involves the workings our from the passage a principle that is true for anyone who belongs to God or a principle for individuals in parallel situations. Legitimate application by the formulation of sound principles is in truth what God has to say to the individual Christian.[111]

Thus, he has two major areas in his hermeneutical principles--principles deriving from biblical studies and principles deriving from the study of the wider cultural context in which these writings originated. In additon, the application of the principles is discussed but only in a limited way.

Fred Fisher, in presenting exegetical principles, does so in nine steps.[112] The first is immediate biblical context followed by textual criticism, translation, and background, by which he means the larger cultural context in which the biblical material originated. He has three steps on the language or words in the Bible--the meaning of words, the form, and the syntax and grammar. Step eight, which Fisher calls study of the theo-

logical motifs, is really an illustration of the
use of exegetical principles enunciated in the
first seven steps. Step nine is entitled "to
make the application to life," but Fisher does not
clarify the process of application.

Fisher's primary emphasis is upon the biblical material itself with some consideration for
the wider cultural context in which this material
was originally produced and used. Most attention
is given to elements of the study of the New Testament itself. Thus, he also has two areas of
emphasis--biblical context and cultural context.
As with Mickelsen, application is discussed but
only in a limited fashion.

Milton S. Terry, author of a nineteenth-
century work on biblical hermeneutics, calls his
work a thesaurus of interpretation.[113] The structure
and development of his material does seem to cover
many areas of hermeneutics. Terry has three parts
in his work: an introduction, a section in which
he discusses the principles of hermeneutics, and
a third section on the history of biblical interpretation. Although Terry has divided his material
rather minutely, which facilitates the finding of
any particular subject, the development of the
material follows a rather general pattern. He discusses the biblical languages per se, the cultural
background of biblical material, figurative language,
and several topics of related material. The specific biblical languages are discussed at some
length in the introduction. The material on
language in the section on principles of hermeneutics deals with the meaning of individual words,
the ideas conveyed by these words, and the biblical
context as a means of discovering what the words
meant. The grammatico-historical sense is discussed
with emphasis upon the study of language and the
study of cultural context. Finally, various figures of speech are discussed. His methodology is
also basically twofold--a study of the Bible itself
and a study of the wider cultural context in which
the biblical material originated.

The survey of principles as set forth by Mickelsen, Fisher, and Terry reveals two major areas of consideration. One is the study of the Bible itself and the other is the study of the historical background of the Bible. These two major areas of context may be labeled biblical context and historical context.[114] The latter refers to the fact that the writer or persons involved in a passage of Scripture lived in a particular cultural context. That is, the religious experience thus recorded had its setting in a specific cultural context. In order to understand the religious experience one must understand the cultural context in which it took place. The cultural context includes everything which made up the experiences of life in the particular period: the mores of the people; the political, economic, geographic, religious, and emotional factors; and so forth. Thus, all the tools by which one understands the cultural context of an ancient time must be brought to bear upon the passage. The biblical context refers to that which may be learned about the religious experience from a study of the Bible itself.

Biblical context may be subdivided into immediate[115] and remote context.[116] Immediate context involves the paragraph in which the scripture is found and the paragraphs immediately preceding and following the passage. The value of immediate biblical context can be seen in an examination of a passage like Deut. 11:18-21. Taken by themselves the expressions "as a sign upon your hand" and "frontlets" may be difficult to understand. But when the whole chapter is read, particularly verse thirteen, these expressions obviously mean to adhere to the commandments of God in all of one's life.[117] Remote context refers to the parts of the Bible which are farther removed from the passage under consideration. Included in remote context is the entire book in which a passage is located and, to some extent, the entire Bible. Thus, parallel passages and parallel ideas also must be considered.[118] For example, a passage dealing with sin must be understood in relationship to what other passages in the Bible say about sin. Genesis 3 is an excellent statement of the Hebrew concept of sin, but Psalm 51 and James 1 (and perhaps other passages) must also be considered if one intends to state a biblical concept of sin.

The importance of context can be seen in a consideration of such practices as prooftexting, scripture memorization, and the kind of biblical study which is most prevalent among Christians. Much biblical study begins with a short passage or even a single verse. Mickelsen has pertinently commented, "The smaller the quantity of material to be interpreted, the greater the danger of ignoring context."[119] As will be shown below, biblical context is of great importance to the layman because of the limited nature of his tools of interpretation.

A further consideration in a discussion of context is what Mickelsen has called the absence of context.[120] However, Mickelsen is talking about the absence of immediate context particularly in the Wisdom literature and the collections of the sayings of Jesus in the Gospels. If immediate context is absent, remote context and even historical context are available to help shed light on a passage.[121]

The survey of the three methodological studies above also reveals other factors in biblical hermeneutics. The very nature of biblical study indicates that it may be so technical that it will tend to confuse and overwhelm the layman. For example, Fisher makes textual studies a step in biblical interpretation. However, textual study is so technical that Fisher virtually writes off this area of biblical study for non-technically trained persons.[122] Yet he says that the honest interpreter cannot ignore textual criticism.[123] In addition, the large number of principles of interpretation (rule of interpretation) set forth by Mickelsen and Terry may easily confuse the layman. Therefore, exegetical principles must be clarified and simplified to as large a degree as possible.

How can complex exegetical principles be simplified for the layman without violating the purpose underlying them--to discover and understand the religious experiences of the people who appear on the pages of the Bible? Perhaps the best way is to set forth the exegetical process step by step so that the interpreter is able to see clearly each part of the process.[124]

If historical interpretion is the first step in interpretation, the interpreter has two choices as to starting place. He can start with cultural context or with biblical context. When the exegetical task is completed, both of these must have been considered to some degree. However, for the layman the Bible itself is the most accessible of the two and the layman probably has more initial interest in the Bible than in cultural context.[125]

Since hermeneutics is circular[126] (interpretation of the part depends upon understanding of the whole and <u>vice versa</u>) it would be advantageous to digest the biblical material all at once. Of course, this is not possible. One must start somewhere, either with the whole or with a part. When starting with the whole, the parts must not be forgotten or ignored. Similarly, when starting with a part, the whole must not be forgotten. Statements such as "the Bible says" may be an example of the first instance, particularly when a general truth or priniciple is being enunciated. Specific statements of the Bible taken out of context may be an example of the latter instance.[127]

Does one start with the whole or with a part in Bible study? The biblical interpreter may consciously start with either one, but adequate interpretation probably involves an interplay of one upon the other. Although the layman most characteristically, perhaps, starts with a single verse or short passage, for the sake of discussion the procedure here will start with the whole and move to the part. A comprehensive perspective of the Bible will better enable the interpreter to place the parts in their proper place.

Starting with the whole Bible focuses attention upon what the interpreter already knows and or thinks about the Bible. Presuppositions or assumptions about the Bible come into view here. Although the subject of presuppositons may seem elementary for the biblical specialist,[128] it is not elementary for the layman.

Mickelsen speaks of the influencing framework of the interpreter and that the interpreter must know the premises of his influencing framework and show that these premises are not "in the least bit contrary to the major emphases and assertions of Scripture."[129] Again the circular nature of interpretation is apparent. Of importance here is the assertion that the interpreter must know what his presuppositions are, that he must be willing to examine them, and that he must be willing for them to be changed if necessary in order best to reflect the nature of Scripture.

The process of interpretation begins with the interpreter and his context--including his presuppositions. The interpreter proceeds to interpret the Bible in its context (exegesis). When the exegetical process is completed, principles are stated which describe the religious experience of the people in the Bible. Finally, these principles are applied to the current context (application).

The importance and influence of presuppositions is of concern here. Every person has presuppostions. To put it in other words, every person has a context out of which he interprets the Bible. Thus, the importance and influence of presupposition can readily be seen. Since everyone has presuppositons, they cannot be ignored. Since they obviously influence one's interpretation of the Bible, the influence must be understood if it is to be controlled. Unless understood and controlled, the influence of one's presuppositions makes eisegesis of Scripture entirely probable.

In considering presuppositions, Bultmann's insights are informative.[130] Of course, Bultmann's existential interpretation leans heavily upon prior understanding. Bultmann affirms that prior understanding is to be brought into one's consciousness and critically tested in his understanding of the text.[131] Further, the result of interpretation is not foreordained by prior understanding. Rather the direction of investigation is made possible.[132] Thus, in order to understand and control the influence of one's presuppositions, one must acknowledge that they exist (attitude), determine what the presuppositions are (identification), and acknowledge that other interpreters with different presuppositions may also have valid interpretations of the Bible. Further, the presuppositions must be tested for validity by one's exegesis of Scripture.

Thus, the concern with presuppositions is related to the circular nature of interpretation. Interpretation must begin from a certain viewpoint--prior understanding in Bultmann's terminology, influencing framework in Mickelsen's terminology. However, the overall viewpoint must be examined in the light of the completed exegesis.[133]

A study of the Bible should be done book by book. Even if one actually begins with a short text, the entire book must be understood to some extent in order to understand adequately the context of the short text. Whether the interpreter engages in a systematic book-by-book examination of the Bible or is teaching Sunday school in which selected short passages are the starting place, the procedure is the same. Study the entire book in which the text is located. Such a study facilitates the understanding of the content of the Bible.[134]

First, rapidly read (or skim) the entire book. If it is short, read the book at one sitting. If, in the longer books, the interpreter needs assistance in locating the major divisions, a dictionary of the Bible may be consulted. But

the best procedure is to read the book for oneself
in a modern translation of the Bible and form some
tentative ideas about the book without outside help.
The point in reading the book rapidly is that one
does not become engaged with the details in the
book but rather gains an impression of the whole
book and its major emphases. Read the book several
times if necessary in order to get an impression
of the whole book.

    Next, outline the book. A subject or descriptive outline is sufficient to start with.
Simply list in the order of appearance in the book
the things which happened or the ideas which appear
in the book. This is particularly easy in a narative book. Facts, persons, institutions, events,
and so forth, are the items of information that
the interpreter looks for in constructing this
outline.[135] The interpreter should not try to be
concise at this point. Write as much information
as is necessary to sketch the book. This procedure will be more difficult in a book like Proverbs.
But even here a grouping of proverbs on similar
subjects can help to clarify the entire book.
After descriptively outlining the book, an interpretative outline should be constructed. In this
procedure the interpreter attempts to interpret
(rather than describe) the facts, persons, events,
institutions, and so forth. The meaning of the
facts in the ancient context are stated.

    In the third step the interpreter should
attempt to state the theme in the book. The theme
may be either a descriptive or interpretative
theme. The descriptive theme would express what
happened. The interpretative theme deals with the
meaning of the things that happened. The interpreter lists the ideas which he feels are expressed in
the book. Again, be full rather than concise.
Among these ideas may be one that captures the
thought of the entire book better than any other.
Probably both themes need to be stated. However,
if the interpreter acquires an understanding of
the Scripture which has any degree of adequacy,
an interpretative theme must be stated.

In the entire exegetical process, the interpreter should write all the ideas and questions that occur to him. Some of the facts, persons, institutions, events, and so forth, may be unfamilar. Information about these items may help to clarify the religious experiences that are presented in the biblical material. Further, information of this kind will help the interpreter to understand more fully the cultural context in which the religious experiences occurred. To secure this information the interpreter, particularly a layman, may consult a dictionary of the Bible. However, the interpreter ought not to use resources other than the Bible itself until the above process has been completed. By completing the exegetical process without using other resources, the interpreter has a fund of understanding that is his own which he may use in evaluating the information from other resources. Thus, he is not entirely dependent upon someone else for his understanding of the Bible.[136]

A comparison of the above process with the process presented by Otto Kaiser[137] shows definite similarities. Kaiser begins with textual criticism and then moves to analysis of the meter. Both steps depend upon a technical knowledge beyond that of most laymen. Thus the layman is dependent from the beginning of his exegetical process upon the prior work of textual critics and translators. Next, Kaiser discusses literary criticism, form criticism, and tradition criticism. Although most layman are not equipped to study these matters in the detail which Kaiser discusses, reading and outlining the biblical material descriptively (with the corollary answering of any questions about facts, persons, institutions, events, and so forth, by use of a dictionary of the Bible) as proposed above is at least the beginning of the process as described by Kaiser. Finally, Kaiser discusses what he calls subject exegesis, concept exegesis, and context exegesis. Subject exegesis deals with "all persons, institutions, and facts of various kinds which are mentioned in the text."[138] Outlining descriptively as presented in the process above deals with the same items. Outlining interpretatively is similar to concept exegesis which Kaiser defines as "understanding of the content of the theological and other leading ideas."[139] Concept exegesis is further defined as throwing "light on the intellectual presuppositions that are taken for granted in the text."[140] Context exegesis has the purpose of making the text live again[141] and is similar to application which will be discussed below under "Principles of Theological Interpretation."

In addition to helping the layman begin the same process which the scholar uses, the method presented above tends to unify the individual books in the Bible and the entire Bible.[142] Further, the method may be used also to interpret the parts of a biblical book or any short text, although the process has been presented in terms of an entire book of the Bible.

## Principles of Theological Interpretation

Previously, the need to separate historical and theological interpretation was asserted for several reasons.[143] The separation of these two elements of the hermeneutical process makes abundantly clear the need to have an intermediate step in the process to bridge the gap between exegesis and application even though some persons object to such an intermediate step.[144] The need for such an intermediate step is further indicated because some students of the Old Testament tend to slide from exegesis to application without saying precisely how the transition was made.[145]

What is the intermediate step between exegesis and application that will make application possible? Stated most simply, the Old Testament must be reduced to principles.[146] To put it another way, exegetical study should already have clarified the religious experience in the passage under consideration. Now the religious experience must be stated in terms of a principle. In this manner the meaning of the biblical passage is put into a

form that can be applied to any other cultural
context including the twentieth century.[147]

On the basis of this concept two questions
must be answered. What kind of principles are to
be discovered in the Old Testament and how are these
principles to be determined? These two questions
bear directly upon one another. The kind of principles must be those which the Old Testament itself
reveals. That is, the Old Testament itself must
provide the principles which will be used as a
guide to interpret the Old Testament and they must
be determined by an inductive study of the Old
Testament. Thus, interpretation of the Old Testament will be circular. Determine the principles
by studying the Old Testament. Use the principles
to interpret the Old Testament.[148]

The contention is made here that the God-
man (man) relationship will provide the kind of
principles that one should derive from Old Testament study. Above all, the Israelite regarded himself in relationship with God and expressed the
God-man relationship as he related to other men
[man (man)]. Repeatedly the writers of the symposium <u>Biblical Authority for Today</u> state that the
relation of God to man and man's response to God
is the central theme of the Bible. The concluding
section states the following presupposition of
Biblical interpretation.

> It is agreed that the primary message of
> the Bible concerns God's gracious and re-
> demptive activity for the saving of sinful
> man that he might create in Jesus Christ
> a people for himself. In this, the Bible's
> central concern and authoritative claim is
> placed upon man and he is called upon to
> respond in faith and obedience throughout
> the whole of his life and work.[149]

H. H. Rowley has stated that the basic unity of the
Bible is to be found in the activity of the independent, sovereign God.[150] Mickelsen shows the
importance of the God-man (man) relationsip by

contrasting the Sitz im Leben and the Sitz im Glauben. No amount of study of the situation in life of the biblical writers will bring the interpreter to the biblical perspective of life in faith. "The position of the biblical writers is that of men in a relationship with God."[151] John Bright says much the same thing when he affirms that the Old Testament has "an amazing continuity with B.C. man" in spite of its discontinuity with the New Testament.[152] Bright contends that the Old Testament contains a typical element which allows it to speak to modern man with immediacy. He affirms that the typical element is essentially the relationship of persons to God and to their fellowmen.

One of the most significant evidences that relationship with God and its consequences is an overriding factor in Old Testament religion is the Mosaic covenant.[153] If, indeed, the covenant reflects the form of ancient Hittite suzerainty treaties,[154] the idea of relationship stands out even more strongly. The ancient Hittite treaties governed the relationship of vassal kings to their overlord and their relationship with each other. The same kind of relationship to God is reflected in the Decalogue. The first four commandments deal with man's relation with God and the last six reflect man's relationship with man. The same factor is evident in other biblical passages as well. The prophet Amos makes abundantly clear that the people were out of relationship with God. God attempted to bring them back into a relationship with himself. But they did not return. Amos said that God caused famine, drought, crop failure, plague, military defeat, and yet the people did not return to him.[155] Other passages make clear that the relationship of God's people to other men is governed by the prior relationship with God.[156]

The following diagram can illustrate the God-man(man) relationship.[157]

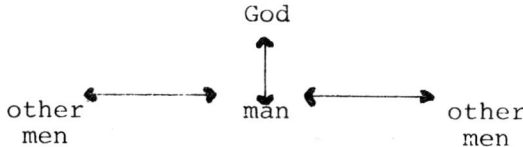

All life is bound up in this concept which forms an overall viewpoint on the basis of which one may interpret the Old Testament. The arrows between God and man in the diagram indicate that it is a mutual and continuing relationship. Likewise, the relationship between a man and other men is a mutual and continuing relationship. The relationship which a man, who is related to God, has with other men is governed by the kind of relationship he has with God.

Although inductive study has been emphasized, some interpreters feel that principles of relationship may be derived directly from the Old Testament. James Smart says that there are many passages which by the nature of their content are likely to be directly meaningful and relevant in the situations of the modern world.

> Samuel's warning to Israel that the concentration of political power in a monarchy may lead to tyranny and to the loss by Israelites of many of the freedoms and priviledges that have been distinctive of their nation can be applied almost directly to a world in which governmental power in many nations has become so colossal that it threatenly overshadows the life of the individual citizen. Amos' attack on the dishonesty of merchants who use false weights and cheat the poor out of a few ounces of every pound of food they buy is directly pertinent to the life of the cities where butchers are found using dishonest scales, most of them usually in the poorer sections of the city. The Fifty-first Psalm can be read by a modern

congregation as its confessions of sin and
plea for God's pardon without any consciousness that the author of that prayer
is separated from them by some thousands
of years and by vast differences in his
cultural situation. We rarely think of
how striking it is that so much in the Old
Testament is immediately comprehensible
and relevant to twentieth-century people.[158]

The quality of immediacy and the fact that the Old
Testament grapples with the questions and problems
which affect any man in any age "is distinctive of
the faith of Israel and arises from the nature of
God whom they worship."[159] On the other hand,
Bright affirms that "there is much in the Old
[Testament] that is strange to the Christian and
that cannot be, and in fact is not, directly a model
for his belief or a law to command his practice."[160]
Bright does not say that there are no teachings in
the Old Testament that cannot be directly a model
for the practice of Christians but the basic thrust
of his entire book leaves no doubt that he feels
such direct models are few and far between if they
exist at all.[161] The positon taken here is that direct application of the Old Testament is probably
possible to only a very limited extent.[162] Direct
application in effect would ignore the fact that
religious experience takes place in a cultural
context. Although religious experience is not
identifiable with the cultural context in which it
occurs, it cannot be understood apart from the
context because the context has influenced and
shaped it. For instance, even the instructions in
the Decalogue, whose application seems so self-
evident, probably need to be understood in the
light of their historical context before they can
be adequately applied and fully appreciated in the
twentieth century.

The first commandment indicates that God's
people are to have no other gods. The usual way
of regarding the commandment is to suppose that
"no other gods' means idols per se. In direct

application the commandment seems to have little
relevance and ignores the element of relationship
between God and man. One should ask further what
bearing idols had upon the God-man relationship.
Since idols as such are not worshipped by many persons in this country, the commandment seemingly can
be ignored. In a similar way, the instruction
about tithing in Malachi is often read directly into
Christian living so that tithing becomes the fulfillment of financial responsibility before God.
In addition, tithers sometimes expect direct financial or other concrete benefits simply because
they tithe.[163] If principles are read directly
from the Old Testament (prior to exegesis) extreme
care must be taken so that the original intent and
purpose is not distorted or changed.

Most often principles of relationship between God and man will be derived from the Old
Testament indirectly through inductive study which
first determines the cultural and biblical context
of the God-man(man) relationship and thus makes
possible the statement of principles. When one
uses the first commandment of the Decalogue in the
context of the ancient Hittite treaties, in which
the king demanded loyalty to himself only and regarded alliances with any other king as detrimental
to his own authority and supremacy, the commandment
takes on new perspective. "No other gods" meant
loyalties and alliances detrimental to loyalty to
God. The vital relationship between God and Israel
was broken or derogated to a role of lesser importance by such alliances.[164]

Although a negative command may not be the
best way to encourage better behaviour, the principles upon which the Ten Commandments are based are
quite as valid today as then. Relationship with
God which is prior in importance to every other
relationship should guide one's behaviour in all
other relationships. When this is placed alongside such admonitions as loving one's neighbor as
oneself and loving as God loves, the Ten Commandments can still be quite meaningful.

The prophets also speak of alliances that are detrimental to one's loyalty to God. Amos preached against taking advantage of the poor and disadvantaged in the community and against unjust social practices such as dishonesty in the use of scales in the market place. Many in Israel had made alliances with these unjust practices. The alliances were inimical to the authority and sovereignty of God in Israel. "No other gods" may mean no entangling alliances of any kind which are detrimental to God's authority in one's life. Evaluated thusly the commandment is very relevant to the twentieth century.

Although reducing the Old Testament to principles means risking the perils of abstraction, the risk must be taken if valid application of the Old Testament is to be possible. However, the risk is decreased if the interpreter keeps the whole process of interpretation constantly before him. The principles derived from the Old Testament have little validity except as they are derived from the real experiences of a real people whose lives were governed by their relationship with God. The principles themselves are not primarily significant. Rather, it is the light they throw upon the God-man (man) relationship which is important. Simply as rules for behavior they are relatively meaningless. Rules for behavior can be derived from other sources. However, the Bible brings enlightenment par excellence concerning the God-man(man) relationships of life. The twentieth-century person can gain such understanding in his own life by reference to principles derived from Old Testament people who also lived in the context of the God-man(man) relationships. Thus, the whole process of interpretation involves the inductive derivation of principles from the historical context of the Old Testament and the application of these principles in the historical context of people living in the twentieth century.

Although specialists are concerned primarily and rightly with their specialty, in the view presented here the work of the specalist is not complete until he has enunciated the principles which can be discovered through his inductive study.165 He may not wish to take the role of the professional and apply the principles to twentieth-century historical situations, but his work is not finished until he has given the professional the tools (that is, the principles) which will allow the professional to make valid applications. Thus, the specialist at least must keep the task of application in view as he pursues his specialty.166

Before illustrating the above method in detail, a diagram of the method may serve to clarify further the process.

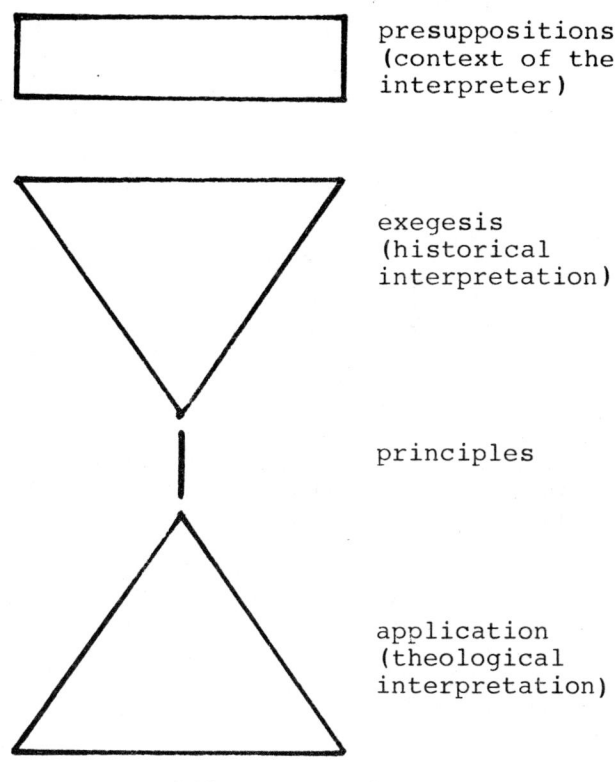

Three of the elements of the diagram (presuppositions, exegesis, application) indicate that interpretation starts with an interpreter and his context, moves to the context of the biblical material, and then to the context of the person or persons to whom application is made.[167] The two triangles representing exegesis and application are pointed toward each other in order to emphasize that interpretation which is aimed at effective application usually is concentrated on a specific biblical passage. Thus, the inverted pyramid representing exegesis signifies that all cultural and biblical information applicable to the passage is directed toward understanding the religious experience in the passage. In interpretation this information has little or no independent value. Similarly, the triangle representing application indicates that many valid applications may flow from an adequate understanding of the religious experience portrayed in the passage. The two triangles are the same size in order to indicate that application is an equally important part of the process of interpretation. Thus, interpretation is not complete until application has been made.[168] Further, since the process is represented as moving from the top to the bottom of the diagram, every other part of the process is to serve the purpose of enabling the interpreter to reach the ultimate goal of interpretation which is application. The gap between the triangles signifies that seldom if ever is direct application possible. The line between the triangles represents the second major step in the process of interpretation as presented here which is the statement of principles based upon careful exegesis of the passage.

The book of Jonah is chosen here for illustrative purposes. A person who is unfamiliar with careful exegetical procedures as presented above should start with a book which has as few problems as possible.[169] The length of the book of Jonah is advantageous for the beginner as is the narrative style of the book.

The role of presuppositons can be seen very

clearly in regard to the book of Jonah. The story of Jonah may be one of the more familiar stories in the Old Testament to many Christians but what is most often remembered is the "great fish." Further, the "great fish" is made the pivotal concept in the story and is often used as a test of orthodoxy.[170] The book of Jonah is thus used in a polemic role as a test of faith usually without any consideration of other emphases in the book. The presuppositions in this case concern the major emphasis and the purpose of the book. The process of exegesis proposed here can be an effective control of such presuppositions. By reading, outlining, and determining the theme of the book, the interpreter can evaluate these preconceptions. Does a firsthand knowledge of the book substantiate or refute the presuppositons?[171]

    Reading the book, several times if necessary, helps give the interpreter a perspective and a grasp of the entire story. At this point details are not as important as the larger elements in the book. A reading of the book of Jonah gives one a sense of Jonah's stubbornness, frustration, and anger with God. Jonah 1:1-3 immediately presents Jonah's unwillingness to go to Nineveh. The experiences during the storm at sea occurred as a result of his unwillingness to go to Nineveh. Although Jonah then undertook the mission to Nineveh, 4:1 makes abundantly clear that he was still reluctant and tremendously frustrated with the results. Because he could not have what he really wanted he became angry with God. Obviously he did not want what God wanted.

    An outline of the book of Jonah helps bring the entire book into sharper focus. At this point the outline should state simply the content of the book without attempting to interpret it.[172] The word of the Lord came to Jonah. Jonah fled from the presence of the Lord. The Lord caused a storm at sea. Jonah admitted that the Lord had caused the storm because he was fleeing from the presence of the Lord. Finally, to save themselves, the crew threw Jonah overboard. God appointed a great

fish by means of which Jonah was saved from the
sea.  Then the word of the Lord came to Jonah a
second time.  So Jonah arose, went to Nineveh, and
preached there.  The city repented and God forgave
the inhabitants.  But it displeased Jonah and he
was angry at God.  He went out of the city to wait
and see what would become of the city.  Then God
appointed a plant to shade Jonah's head.  When the
plant died, Jonah was angry for the plant.  Then
God said, "You pity the plant.  Should I not pity
Nineveh?"

    The task of interpretation becomes more
difficult at this point although in the book of
Jonah the biblical material itself seems to give
the interpretation that is intended.  If the above
outline has been done thoroughly and extensively,
a convenient step at this point is to condense the
content outline and begin to describe what happened
in interpretative statements.  That is, condensation
of the content outline will enable the interpreter
to view the content of the book more easily.  Then
a descriptive or interpretative outline in terms
of religious experience needs to be made.[173]  Condensing the above outline may result in the following statement:  Jonah was called twice to go to
Nineveh and preach in the city; finally he went and
the city repented; Jonah was angry at God because
of this; God asked Jonah if his anger was justified
and then demonstrated that it was not justified.
Interpretatively, the following statements may be
made:  Jonah did not want to preach in Nineveh
because he felt they should be punished instead of
forgiven (Jonah hated the Ninevites and let his
hatred come between them and the mercy of God);
God tried to teach him that his anger was not
justified and that even a hated people have the
right to repent and be forgiven (God's mercy is
available to anyone regardless of how the person
who already belongs to God may feel about it).

    Already a theme has been suggested in the
statements used above to express what happened in
the book of Jonah.  God wanted to show mercy to
Nineveh and Jonah did not want him to do it.  In

other words, the mercy of God is displayed in a particular circumstance, and more information may be needed before the interpreter is ready to apply the idea of the mercy of God to another circumstance. Some pertinent questions may be raised at this point. Why did Jonah hate Nineveh so much? Why is Nineveh singled out as the recipient of God's mercy? Of course, a most pertinent question concerns the historicity of the fish swallowing Jonah. Materials other than the Bible may need to be consulted in order to answer these and other questions. Because of its comprehensive nature an excellent starting place for the layman is a dictionary of the Bible.

One learns that Nineveh represented not only the oppression imposed by war lords of the Near East but also the immorality, viciousness, and irreligion of the Gentile world. With this information Jonah's hatred at least becomes understandable. However, the book of Jonah makes clear that Jonah's hatred was still not justifiable because God did not feel that way. If such a people (in current terminology, the worst sinners you can find) are legitimate targets of God's mercy, anyone is eligible for God's mercy. Although the historicity of the story has not yet been considered, the above information lends weight to the theme of the book which was stated above.

When historicity is considered other questions arise. What of the miracles in this book and the entire Bible for that matter, particularly Jesus' miracles? Does Jesus' use of the story of Jonah (Matt. 12:39-41) and his apparently regarding it as historical force Christians today to the same viewpoint? Obviously, one's presuppositons about the entire Bible are of concern here. Further, if one rejects the historicity of the book of Jonah, is its validity for the Christian necessarily destroyed, and is its apparent purpose of showing the availability of God's mercy to any person thereby negated? Again, the question of validity may engage one's presuppositions. However, the book has been interpreted as a parable and from this point of view one may legitimately conclude that Jonah "still remains unmistakably a portrait of the narrow and intolerant Hebrew of Ezra's day, who refuses to face the universalistic implications of the divine revelation and its call to world mission."[174]

Since the exegetical task is to understand the religious experience [God-man(man) relationship] in the biblical material, this experinece should be definitely stated. The book of Jonah portrays Jonah deliberately excluding Nineveh from his concern because of his hatred. God attempted to teach him that this was wrong because it denied God's mercy to them and God's mercy is available to anyone. Now the task of stating this experience in the form of a principle must be undertaken. Jonah is the central figure in the book and the principles may be stated from his viewpoint: A Christian must not deliberately exclude anyone from God's mercy. However, God's viewpoint is prominent in the book and a corollary principle may be stated from that viewpoint: God's mercy is available to anyone. Of course, the biblical position seems to insist that God works through his people. Thus, his mercy is available only as his people make it available. The first statement of principle above is from a negative viewpoint. Stated positively, and emphasizing the responsibility of God's people, it may read: Christians must make the mercy of God available to everyone.[175]

These may not exhaust the principles that may be derived from the book of Jonah but are sufficient to illustrate the procedure. Application of these principles may be made to many situations. Here the suggestion of Toombs is especially pertinent.

> How the application is made cannot be determined in advance. Its structure must arise out of the minister's pastoral experience. He knows his congregation, the problems they face and the temptations that press upon them. All the wisdom pro-

vided by his parish work and all his knowledge of the contemporary world are brought to bear on the Scripture.[176]

The point seems to be that, just as exegesis begins with a concrete historical situation, so also does application. The application of principles very definitely assumes a new historical situation. The principles are valid only as a means of bridging the gap between then and now. The point is not that they have no validity as general principles in and of themselves. Rather, the purpose of God as seen in the God-man(man) relationships in the Old Testament is to elicit a response from man. The God-man relationship is expected to have an effect upon the lives of people today. An effect can take place only in a concrete historical situation. As far as interpretation of the Old Testament is concerned, principles derived from an exegesis of the Old Testament are valid only as they are applied to a new historical situation.

However, some possible situations may be envisioned as a means of illustration. A church may exclude people from the mercy of God for reasons as inadequate as Jonah's hatred of Nineveh. Some people may be exluded from the mercy of God on the basis of race. Some Christians on either end of the "liberal-conservative" theological continuum may exclude persons on the other end from the mercy of God because of the difference in theological views. On the other hand, in a society in which a church may often represent a certain social stratum, Christians need the reminder that they are obligated to extend the mercy of God to all people because God intends for it to be available to all people.

The interpretative task as presented here involves more than a knowledge of the Bible. A knowledge of the Bible is an integral part of the process of exegesis. Certainly it plays an important part in the process of application. However, in application other elements are also at work. In order to exegete adequately, the interpreter must know the ancient historical situation of the biblical material as well as possible. Similarly, in order to apply adequately the interpreter needs to know the present historical situation as well as possible--people, issues, and so forth. Further, in order to elicit a response to God, the interpreter, who most characteristically is a pastor, must make use of the art of public speaking, of psychology, and perhaps information and knowledge from other fields also.[177]

The solution suggested here is a rational approach. Although faith is a very important part of the life of God's people, faith is observable only in the actions and words of God's people. Only when the observable phenomena have been investigated as thoroughly as biblical scholarship permits can some estimate be made of what these phenomena meant in terms of the faith of the people involved. That is, only by understanding the context in which the religious experience occurred can the experience be understood. If the suggestion of Haller[178] is taken seriously, the interpreter may come very close to imposing upon the Old Testament his subjective presuppositons. In discussing the possibility of a deeper meaning in Scripture, Bright takes a position similar to the position presented in this paper. If there is such a meaning, it is not open to exegetical procedures.[179] However, faith that the Bible is the authoritative word of God is needed in the application of principles discovered by the method suggested above.

The solution suggested above clearly and visibly separates historical interpretation from theological interpretation thus enabling the interpreter to understand the process of interpretation more easily. But the solution also pulls historical and theological interpretation together by emphasizing that they are both parts of the same process. Neither is adequate without the other.[180]

By its emphasis upon discovering principles in the Old Testament the method suggested above emphasizes that there are some things in the Old

Testament that cannot apply in the twentieth-century. At the same time, the logical end of determining principles is to make some kind of application to people living in the twentieth century. The process by which principles may be determined makes possible a feasible means of determining what in the Old Testament is binding on Christians and what is not. Further, the assumption that both Testaments demonstrate the same religion emphasizes the unity of the Testaments. Jesus may be considered the end of revelation or the apex of revelation but not because he reveals something that was not revealed to God's people earlier. Rather, he is the fullness of revelation because he clarifies what was revealed earlier.

The method suggested above reduces the complexity and technicality of the specialist to proportions manageable by the layman without, however, derogating the technicality of the specialist to the role of uselessness. Thus, no gap in methodology is raised between the specialist and the layman. The layman who uses this methodology and understands that it is only a simplification of the technology of the specialist will have greater appreciation for the specialist, for his work, and for the results of his work. At the same time, interpretation which is seen as a process ending in application can help the specialist have a greater appreciation for the needs and purposes of the Church at large in its use of the Bible.

Since the interpretative process described above has been presented in terms of its use by laymen, it may be helpful to make some suggestions concerning other tools that the layman may be able to use in addition to an adequate study Bible. The layman probably has limitations of money, time, and training. Most laymen probably will not buy many tools for biblical interpretation. Further, the layman does not have the time or training to make the detailed study that the use of some tools demands. In consideration of these limitations the tools must contain as much information as possible in relation to their cost. Probably, also, most laymen will not use extensive discussions that are highly technical. Since the emphasis of the method above has been upon context and an overall viewpoint in approaching the Bible, perhaps the most important tool for the layman will be a dictionary of the Bible. An adequate Bible dictionary will provide materials giving insight into the cultural context of the Bible and an overall viewpoint of individual books of the Bible (including outline and theme). A bible dictionary will also contain articles of a general nature which will help the layman gain an overall viewpoint of the Bible. An atlas of the Bible will enhance this general knowledge. At the same time, a dictionary of the Bible will provide articles on specific subjects and persons in the Bible thus assisting the layman to interpret shorter passages of scripture. An introduction to the Old Testament, particularly the sections on canon and text, can facilitate the overall approach to the Old Testament. More specific study of words and ideas can be enhanced by a careful use of a concordance and commentaries.[181]

The purpose of interpretation is to understand the religious experience of the people who populate the Bible and to transmit the meaning of that experience to persons in the twentieth century.[182] The methodology above facilitates this purpose by making explicit the various steps in the process of interpretation. The task of interpretation must begin by throwing as much light on the passage as possible. However, this task begins with an interpreter. Thus, the process of interpretation leads from the situation of the interpreter to the ancient situation represented in the Bible to the present historical situation of the person or persons to whom application of the passage is made.

¹Although historical and theological hermeneutics need to be separated in order to clarify each, they are in a sense inseparable as A. Berkeley Mickelsen, Interpreting the Bible (Philadelphia: Westminster Press, 1963), pp. 56-57, and Smart, Interpretation, p. 43, show. Mickelsen further demonstrates the inseparability of exegesis and application in his discussion of the inseparability of event and interpretation, pp. 60-65, especially p. 62.

²Bright states explicitly in his methodological critique, Early Israel in Recent History Writing, p. 114,
"The history of Israel. . . is not the history of a Twelve-Clan League, nor of a nation; it is the history of a faith and its people. . . . /This/ is another way of saying that the history of Israel and the history of Israel's religion are one and the same topic."
Cf. Bright, Authority, p. 170.

³G. Ernest Wright, "Old Testament Scholarship in Prospect," p. 185. Cf. John Bright, "An Exercist in Hermeneutics," Interpretation, XX (April, 1966), 189-90; Bright, Authority, p. 170; Smart, Dialogue, p. 137.

⁴"Theological Education in Trouble," Christianity Today, XI (March 17, 1967), 26. Cf. with the roughly opposite viewpoint of Morton Smith, "The Present State of Old Testament Studies," Journal of Biblical Literature, LXXXVIII (March, 1969), 19-35.

⁵See below, pp. 123-132.

⁶Bright, Authority, pp. 177-82.

⁷Cf. the example of Wellhausen and Barth above, Chapter I.

⁸Clarence T. Craig, "Biblical Theology and the Rise of Historicism," Journal of Biblical

Literature, LXII (December, 1943), 294. These emphases can be seen clearly by comparing such introductions to the Old Testament as Bentzen's and that by Bernhard W. Anderson, Understanding the Old Testament (2nd ed.; Englewood Cliffs, N. J.: Prentice-Hall, Inc., 1966).

⁹ Cf. Ramm, Protestant Biblical Interpretation, p. 117. "A given passage . . . has one meaning, but the moral principles of the passage may be capable of many applications. We must keep in mind that applications are not interpretations and must not receive that status."

¹⁰ See above, pp. 2-3.

¹¹ John Reumann, "Introduction," Biblical Problems and Biblical Preaching, C. K. Barrett, Biblical Series Number 6, reprint of Foundery Pamphlet Number 7 (Philadelphia: Fortress Press, 1964), p. v, states,
> "All too often the scholars, even those engaged in biblical research, have not seemed concerned about the preacher's task. On the other side of the coin, all too frequently among preachers there has been an uneasy feeling that their current sermons might not pass muster on the basis of what they had learned at seminary, let alone on the basis of more recent exegetical and theological insights."

The necessity for bringing scholars and laymen closer together has been recognized by scholars. See James L. Price, review of A New Testament History: The Story of the Emerging Church by Floyd V. Filson, in Journal of Biblical Literature, LXXXV (June, 1966), 241, who says,
> "Most scholars are understandably disinterested in translating for nonspecialists the results of their own or other's research. Besides studies, and the expectations of colleagues, they may feel that popularization is a task for the religion journalist or the professional writer of church school literature. Yet something

more than this is needed, unless there
increase among us 'the cultured despisers
of religion.'"

On the same theme James N. Settle, Executive Associate of the American Council of Learned Societies, in addressing the Society of Biblical Literature in December, 1968, "The Learned Society in America: Responsibilities and Opportunities," Bulletin of the American Academy of Religion, VI (Summer, 1969), 5-6, said,

"There remains within some of the humanistic disciplines a tendency for scholars
to stand aloof from the pedagogical concerns of the field. . . . We smirk at the
lack of substantive training in the schools
of education--while their products teach
our children and train our students. . . .
The scholarly, prestigious organization
within a discipline must commit itself
actively to solving whatever problems exist, from the high school level through
doctoral research."

[12] Reumann, "Introduction," Biblical Problems and Biblical Preaching, p. vii.

[13] Smart, Interpretation, pp. 40-44.

[14] Ibid., pp. 42-43.

[15] Bright, Authority, seems to make just such a distinction between the Testaments. See pp. 57, 183, 200. On p. 183, he says,

"The Old Testament is different in that it
was not in the first instance a document
of the Church at all: it was not written
by Christians for Christians. The more
seriously we take it in its plain meaning,
the more clearly we see that it is
the document of a religion genetically related to our own, yet not precisely the
same as our own. It is a document of the
faith of old Israel, and only secondarily
a document of the Church."

In addition, Bright affirms that the significance of the Old Testament is largely pedagogic. However, Bright is not Marcionist in attempting to let preaching from the Old Testament be governed by the New Testament. Bright affirms that the God of the Old Testament is our God. See p. 207. Fred Fisher, How to Interpret the New Testament (Philadelphia: Westminster Press, 1967), pp. 21, 88-89, also relegates the Old Testament to a minor position. Cf. also the discussion of existentialism above, pp. 105-19.

[16] See Bright, Authority, pp. 185-87, for examples.

[17] Bright, Authority, pp. 184-96, describes various ways in which the unity of the Testaments may be regarded: as parity, as developmental, as propaedeutic, as Heilsgeschichte.

[18] Cf. Bright, Authority, p. 18. Bright asks, "How are these ancient laws, institutions, and concepts, these ancient narratives, sayings, and expressions of an ancient piety, actually to be taken as authoritative over the faith and life of the Christian?" Also see above, Chapter I, the statement of the problem.

[19] Bright, Authority, p. 57, Cf. pp. 183, 200.

[20] Cf. ibid., pp. 78, 138.

[21] Mickelsen, Interpreting the Bible, p. 91.

[22] Ibid., p. 89.

[23] Rowley, The unity of the Bible, p. 8.

[24] Genesis 3; Psalm 51; Rom. 3:23; James 1:12-15.

[25] Paul indicates that Abraham was saved by faith not by works. Romans 4.

[26] Rowley, The Unity of the Bible, pp. 19-121.

[27] Bright, Authority, p. 140.

[28] David Noel Freedman, "The Interpretation of Scripture: On Method in Biblical Studies: The Old Testament," Interpretation, XVII (July, 1963), 315. Cf. Bright's statement above, p. 127, n. 1.

[29] Rowley, The Unity of the Bible, p. 28.

[30] Mickelsen, Interpreting the Bible, p. 103.

[31] Freedman, "Interpretation of Scripture," p. 315.

[32] Bright, Authority, p. 210.

[33] Cf. Lawrence E. Toombs, The Old Testament in Christian Preaching (Philadelphia: The Westminster Press, 1961), p. 26. Cf. Bultmann, "Significance," p. 32.

[34] Rowley, The Unity of the Bible, p. 186.

[35] Cf. the viewpoint expressed by Henry Jackson Flanders, Jr., Robert Wilson Crapps, and David Anthony Smith, People of the Covenant, An Introduction to the Old Testament (New York: The Ronald Press Company, 1963), pp. 167-68.

[36] Cf. C. F. D. Moule, "Revelation," IDB, IV, 55.

[37] H. Wheeler Robinson, Inspiration and Revelation in the Old Testament (Oxford: Clarendon Press, 1946), pp. 271-82.

[38] Michael Polanyi, Personal Knowledge (Chicago: The University of Chicago Press, 1958).

[39] Ibid., pp. vii-viii.

[40] Ibid., pp. 17, 312.

[41] Ibid., pp. vii, 300-303, 311.

[42] Smart, Interpretation, p. 161. See partic-

ularly chapters 6 and 7 on inspiration and authority.

[43] Rylaarsdam, "The Problem of Faith and History in Biblical Interpretation," pp. 27-28, also voices the dynamic concept of revelation:
"The most distinctive feature of the current theological emphasis is its dynamic view of revelation. . . . Revelation is not a static form with a stable content. subject to descriptive analysis: it is a dynamic action existentially apprehended, the source of faith and inspired reponse."

[44] Smart, Interpretation, p. 168.

[45] Ibid., p. 195.

[46] Bernard Ramm, The Pattern of Religious Authority (Grand Rapids, Mich.: Wm. B. Eerdmans Publishing Co., 1959), p. 19.

[47] Ibid., p. 21.

[48] Ibid., p. 29. Underlining and parentheses his.

[49] Smart, Interpretation, p. 43. Cf. Daniel Lys, The Meaning of the Old Testament (Nashville: Abingdon Press, 1967), p. 147: "Understanding and appropriation are two different concerns." Cf. Mickelsen, Interpreting the Bible, pp. 3-4.

[50] Cf. Moule, "Revelation," p. 57.

[51] Bright, Authority, p. 207, affirms that the Old Testament is able to address modern man with immediacy because of its humanity, because of "its hopes and aspirations, its piety and sin," because of "the way in which its people understand and respond to the claims of their God." He also states that the Old Testament "is typical because human nature remains essentially unchanged and because men do find themselves in typical situations and react to circumstances, their fellow men, and

their God in typical ways."

[52] Stendahl, "Biblical Theology," p. 428.

[53] Bright, Authority, p. 159.

[54] Stendahl, "Biblical Theology," p. 429, "Do these old writings have any meaning beyond their significance as sources for the past? . . . The answer rests on the act of faith by which Israel and its sister by adoption, the church, recognizes its history as sacred history, and finds in these writings the epitome of the acts of God. As such these writings are meaningful to the church in any age."

[55] Bright, Authority, p. 169. Cf. above, pp. 124-26.

[56] Cf. Toombs, The Old Testament in Christian Preaching, p. 13; Bright, Authority, p. 169.

[57] Markus Barth, Conversation with the Bible, p. 306.

[58] The three suggested solutions surveyed below are only a sampling of recent attempts to solve the problem of the relevance of the Old Testament to the Christian faith. See also Lys, The Meaning of the Old Testament; Markus Barth, Coversation with the Bible. Interpretation magazine presents a series of articles on this subject beginning with John Bright, "An Exercise in Hermeneutics," Interpretation, XX (April, 1966), 188-210. Cf. "Editorial," Interpretation, XX(April, 1966), 229, for an explanation of this series.

[59] Harvey H. Guthrie, Jr., Israel's Sacred Songs (New York: The Seabury Press, 1966), p. 197.

[60] Ibid., pp. vii, 25.

[61] Ibid., p. 200.

[62] Ibid., p. 202.

[63] Ibid., p. 201.

[64] Ibid.

[65] Ibid., p. 203.

[66] Smart, Interpretation; Dialogue.

[67] Smart, Dialogue, p. 136.

[68] Ibid., p. 12.

[69] Ibid., p. 14. This statement can be contrasted with a similar statement by Bright. "The structure of the New Testament's theology is essentially the same as that of the Old, but with the content radically transformed in the light of what Christ has done." Bright, Authority, p. 148. Underlining in both quotations is that of the authors.

[70] Smart, Dialogue, p. 135.

[71] Ibid., p. 52.

[72] Ibid., p. 32.

[73] Ibid., p. 44.

[74] Ibid., pp. 137-38.

[75] Bright, Authority, p. 18.

[76] Bright discusses two kinds of authority and affirms the former as a norm of what was originally held: something to compel belief.

[77] Bright, Authority, pp. 84-85.

[78] Ibid., p. 106.

[79] Ibid., p. 105.

[80] Ibid., p. 110.

[81] Ibid., pp. 91, 110-12.

[82] Ibid., p. 112.

[83] Ibid.

[84] Ibid., p. 115. This is similar to the definition given by Stendahl, "Biblical Theology," and by Dentan, Preface to Old Testament Theology, pp. 122-25.

[85] Bright, Authority, p. 124.

[86] Ibid., p. 130.

[87] Ibid., p. 138.

[88] Ibid., p. 148; underlining his.

[89] Ibid., pp. 168-73.

[90] Ibid., p. 173; underlining his.

[91] See ibid., p. 203, for examples in which Bright attempts to show how the Christian may find meaning in the Old Testament and in which he does slide from exegesis to application.

[92] Ibid., p. 197.

[93] Ibid., p. 210.

[94] See below, "Principles of Theological Interpretation," pp. 142-158.

[95] Bright, Authority pp. 213-51; see also p. 209.

[96] Ibid., p. 218.

[97] Cf. ibid., pp. 77f, 138, 140.

[98] Ibid., p. 112.

[99] Ibid., p. 148.

[100] Ibid., p. 200; cf. p. 183.

[101] Ibid., p. 184; cf. pp. 197-98, 212.

[102] Guthrie, *Israel's Sacred Songs*, pp. vii, 25.

[103] Smart, *Dialogue*, p. 14.

[104] Bright, *Authority*, p. 148.

[105] David H. Kelsey, Review of *The Authority of the Old Testament* by John Bright, *Journal of Biblical Literature*, LXXXVI (June, 1967), 217-18; underlining his.

[106] Smart, *Dialogue*, p. 137; Bright, *Authority*, chapter 3, expecially p. 159.

[107] Mickelsen, *Interpreting the Bible*, see Table of Contents.

[108] Ibid., pp. 99-113.

[109] Ibid., p. 178.

[110] Cf. ibid., p. 350.

[111] Ibid., p. 357, underlining his.

[112] Fisher, *How to Interpret the New Testament*.

[113] Terry, *Biblical Hermeneutics*, p. 1.

[114] The discussion of modern critical interpretation, above, pp. 65-78, especially pp. 68-69, also points to these two areas of consideration in biblical studies.

[115] Mickelsen, *Interpreting the Bible*, pp. 102-4.

[116] This term is used by Terry, *Biblical Hermeneutics*, p. 210. Cf. Mickelsen, *Interpreting the Bible*, pp. 99-113.

[117] Dt. 11:13 states, "Obey my commandments which I command you this day, to love the Lord your God, and to serve him with all your heart and with all your soul." From the Revised Standard Version of the Bible, copyrighted 1946, 1952 ©1971, 1973.

[118] Cf. Mickelsen's differentiation of these terms, Interpreting the Bible, pp. 104-12.

[119] Ibid., p. 113.

[120] Ibid., pp. 112-13.

[121] Some immediate context is probably present, however, even in the Wisdom literature and in the sayings of Jesus. The particular combination of proverbs and sayings probably forms a kind of immediate context which should not be ignored.

[122] Fisher, How to Interpret the New Testament, pp. 63-65. The book is addressed to beginners, which would presumably include laymen.

[123] Ibid., p. 52.

[124] It is understood here that these steps are presented for the layman and that the specialist can pursue each step more intensively. However, the steps remain essentially the same for both.

[125] Even the biblical specialist must hold the Bible itself as his ultimate concern. Note, for example, the viewpoint of G. Ernest Wright whose major effort has been in the area of understanding the cultural context of the Old Testament. He has said, in The Old Testament and Theology (New York: Harper & Row, Publishers, 1969), p. 9, that the Old Testament must be taken "as . . . of serious moment for present faith and life."

[126] The circular nature of interpretation is presented in the ecumenical symposium on interpretation, Biblical Authority for Today, ed. by Alan Richardson and W. Schweitzer (London: SCM Press,

Ltd., 1951), pp. 130-31.
> "To set out rules of interpretation means asking the question: What are the methods of interpretation that are best fitted to the whole of the biblical message? Hence, we must already understand this message as a whole before we can set out rules for interpreting the single text. The consequence of this logical circle is that in fact interpretation of Scripture and rules for its interpretation must always mutually enrich and correct each other."

See also Bernard L. Ramm, "Biblical Interpretation," in Baker's Dictionary of Practical Theology, ed. by Ralph G. Turnbull (Grand Rapids, Mich.: Baker Book House, 1967), pp. 105-6, who cites Bultmann's existential understanding of exegesis as another version of the hermeneutical circle.

[127] Cf. above, p. 136.

[128] Presuppositions have a vast amount of importance for the specialist also. For example, Bright, A History of Israel, has quite different presuppositions about the patriarchal period than Noth, The History of Israel. Wright comments in "Modern Issues in Biblical Studies," p. 295, that before the teacher can instruct in this part of the Bible he must come to some conclusion about these presuppositions.

[129] Mickelsen, Interpreting the Bible, p. 19.

[130] See above, pp. 92-93.

[131] Bultmann, "The Problem of Hermeneutics," pp. 253-54.

[132] Ibid., pp. 255-56.

[133] Cf. Barr's discussion of presuppositions, Old and New in Interpretation, pp. 171-92.

[134] Cf. Mickelsen, Interpreting the Bible, pp. 100-102.

[135] Many modern versions of the Bible have such descriptive statements as paragraph or chapter headings. However, these statements must be used with caution because the reader may depend upon them to such an extent that he does not study the Bible himself. In addition, these statements are sometimes interpretative rather than descriptive.

[136] Cf. Otto Kaiser, "Old Testament Exegesis," Exegetical Method, trans. by E. V. N. Goetchius (New York: The Seabury Press, 1967), p. 17.

[137] Ibid., pp. 11-32. Kaiser's methodology is chosen for comparison because it is presented from the point of view of the scholar and is designed for professionals.

[138] Ibid., p. 24.

[139] Ibid., p. 26.

[140] Ibid., p. 31.

[141] Ibid., p. 32.

[142] The procedure presented here is very close to the procedure of Donald G. Miller, "How to Study the Bible," Introduction to the Bible, Vol. I of The Layman's Bible Commentary, ed. by Balmer H. Kelly (25 vols.; Richmond, Va.: John Knox Press, 1959), pp. 143-71. Fisher has a similar procedure, How to Interpret the New Testament, pp. 31-39. Cf. Mickelsen, Interpreting the Bible, p. 100. An illustration of the method presented above is given below under "Principles of Theological Interpretation."

[143] Above, pp. 111-114.

[144] Eduard Haller, "On the Interpretative Task," Interpretation, XXI (April, 1967), 163, says,
"I can walk the road of exegesis rightly only if I open no gap between historical and theological exegesis which would create a need for emergency bridges, and if

>       I resist the temptation of divorcing in-
>   tellectual activity and the listening atti-
>   tude of faith."

Cf. Millar Burrows, "The Task of Biblical Theology," Journal of Bible and Religion, XIV (February, 1946), 14, who speaks of a gap between the critical activities of biblical scholarship (in the areas of history, literature, and exegesis) and the everyday used of the Bible in the church. He affirms the need to span this gap. Cf. also Smart, Interpretation, p. 36, where he says,

>   "When the historian has done his work con-
>   scientiously and the gap between the world
>   of the Bible and the world of our day has
>   become a gaping chasm, the church with full
>   right demands that scholarship go a stage
>   further, bridge this chasm, and show how
>   the word of the Bible in spite of its time-
>   bound quality is still a word of God to man
>   in the present day."

[145]See above, pp. 123-132.

[146]Fisher, How to Interpret the New Testament, p. 168; Mickelsen, Interpreting the Bible, pp. 357-60; Ramm, Protestant Biblical Interpretation, p. 117. None of these writers, however, discuss in detail what this step involves. Cf. also Smart, Interpretation, p. 38. John Marsh, "History and Interpretation," Biblical Authority for Today, p. 196, says that in the historical situation of the Bible we must try to penetrate beyond the historically relevant forms of experience to the essential demands of God and the manner of man's response.

[147]Mickelsen, Interpreting the Bible, p. 357, states,
>   "Personal application involves the working

out from the passage a principle that is true for anyone who belongs to God or a principle for individuals in parallel situations."

[148] See the discussion above, pp. 137-139.

[149] Biblical Authority for Today, p. 240. Cf. pp. 157-58, 166, 197, 218, 229, 236.

[150] Rowley, The Unity of the Bible, p. 98n.

[151] Mickelsen, Interpreting the Bible, p. 163.

[152] Bright, Authority, p. 207.

[153] Cf. Toombs, The Old Testament in Christian Preaching, pp. 17-18, 50-55. He goes to the prophetic movement for evidence of the God-man relationship.

[154] G. E. Mendenhall, "Covenant," IDB, I, 714-23. Morton Smith in "The Present State of Old Testament Studies," pp. 25-32, especially p. 30, notes some reasons why Mendenhall's view may not be entirely adequate.

[155] Amos 4:6-11.

[156] Cf. Pss. 15; 24. Psalm 1, which some regard as a preface to the book of Psalms, speaks primarily of relationship with God.

[157] Cf. Toombs' diagram, The Old Testament in Christian Preaching, p. 52. Mickelsen, Interpreting the Bible, p. 358, expresses a similar viewpoint when he says the reader, in order to make a real application of the Bible, must ask himself a four-part question: What in the passage applies to "(1) a believer's relationship to God? (2) a believer's relationship to other believers? (3) a believer's relationship to unbelievers? (4) a believer's responsibility for himself--personal outlook, attitude, growth, endeavors to avoid defeat and to achieve maturity?"

[158] Smart, Dialogue, p. 74.

[159] Ibid., p. 75.

[160] Bright, Authority, p. 110.

[161] Ibid., p. 141. The viewpoints of Smart and Bright concerning the possibility that the Old Testament may be directly relevant seem to be based on a stronger leaning toward unity in the case of Smart and a stronger leaning toward disunity in the case of Bright. The differences between the Old Testament and the New Testament indicate that the Old Testament cannot be applied directly to Christians today. On the other hand, the unity of the Testaments seems to support the possibility of some kind of application of the Old Testament to the twentieth century. If one bridges the gap between exegesis and application, a viable way of conceiving the unity of the Testaments may be suggested also.

[162] Cf. Biblical Authority for Today, p. 243.

[163] Cf. Bright's discussion of tithing, Authority, p. 54.

[164] Cf. Mark 10:17-31 (Luke 18:18-30; Matt. 19:16-30). The commandments dealing with man's relationship to God seem conspicuously absent. Apparently, the young man did not have an adequate relationship with God.

[165] Cf. Kaiser, "Old Testament Exegesis," Exegetical Method, p. 32.

[166] James Smart seems to say that the specialist should indeed be concerned with the role of the professional, Interpretation, pp. 38-39, when he says that
"the determination of what the text means for man now has been regarded as merely the task of applying in present-day life the truths and principles that have been laid bare by the historical investigation, a task that can safely be left in the hands

of preachers and professors of homiletics. . . . (Specialists) need to ask themselves why so many ministers, who have been trained to read the Bible historically and critically during their years in college and seminary, find themselves at a loss to know how to make its contents meaningful to the people to whom they minister. Preachers and teachers become lost in the chasm that scholarship has left gaping open between the original and the contemporary situation." (Underlining his.) Cf. the statement of the problem in Chapter I. Above.

167 Cf. Mickelsen, Interpreting the Bible, pp. 129, 169-72.

168 Cf. Kaiser, "Old Testament Exegesis," Exegetical Method, p. 9.

169 Of course, the great fish in the book of Jonah may present a problem for the interpreter. However, the method described here, if used carefully, can overcome this problem.

170 William Neil, "Jonah, Book of," IDB, II, 964.

171 Of course, this procedure assumes that the interpreter wishes to recognize and evaluate his presuppositions.

172 Frank Stagg, "An Analysis of the Book of James," Review and Expositior, LXVI (Fall, 1969), 366, contrasts an interpretative outline with an outline which only reveals the content of the book. A content outline may very well use the words of the text itself.

173 Condensation of the content outline already involves interpretation because the interpreter must decide what elements of the content of the book will appear in the condensed outline. Obviously, these will receive greater emphasis than the omitted details.

[174]Neil, "Jonah, Book of," p. 967. Although the book of Jonah has been interpreted allegorically, the allegorical method is ruled out in this discussion because of the deficiencies given above, pp. 37-43.

[175]Peter's experience with Cornelius in Acts 10 seems pertinent. Peter concluded, "I perceive that God shows no partiality, but in every nation any one who fears him and does what is right is acceptable to him." From the Revised Standard Version of the Bible, Copyrighted 1946, 1952 © 1972, 1973.

[176]Toombs, The Old Testament in Christian Preaching, p. 21.

[177]Cf. H. C. Brown, Jr., A Quest for Reformation in Preaching (Waco, Texas: Word Books, 1968), pp. 28-29.

[178]Haller, "On the Interpretative Task," p. 163. See above, p. 142.

[179]Bright, Authority, pp. 93-94. This contradicts Raymond E. Brown's view of sensus plenior. See above, pp. 81-87.

[180]Ramm, "Biblical Interpretation," p. 106, emphasizes the essential unity of the interpretative process.

[181]Information on use of such tools may be found in Balmer H. Kelly and Donald G. Miller, eds., Tools for Bible Study (Richmond, Va.: John Knox Press, 1956) and Frederick W. Danker, Multipurpose Tools for Bible Study (St. Louis: Concordia Publishing House, 1966). Though these books were written for professionals, they may help laymen also.

[182]Cf. Mickelsen, Interpreting the Bible, p. 5; Bright, Authority, p. 18.

## CHAPTER V

## IMPLICATIONS OF THE RELEVANCE OF THE OLD TESTAMENT FOR THE CHRISTIAN FAITH

The implications suggested below are not necessarily in any logical order. Since all of theology is interrelated, a methodology of biblical interpretation may have far-reaching implications. The purpose here, however, is not to be exhaustive but rather suggestive.

A primary implication is the relevance of the Old Testament for the Christian faith. This study was initiated in order to show that the Old Testament is relevant for Christians today. Two answers are necessary to indicate that the Old Testament is relevant. Yes, it is relevant because Christians believe it is relevant. To answer in this way is to say that Christians believe in the Old Testament. The Old Testament is regarded as authoritative by most Christians. But this does not mean that Christians use it in a way which has utilitarian relevance for their lives. To believe in it is not the same thing as using it. The second answer is that it can be relevant in a practical way if it is interpreted adequately. The first answer emphasizes the strong role which faith plays in the relevance of the Old Testament. Christians believe the Old Testament has value although they may not know what the value is or how to realize it in their lives. This study is directly related to the second answer. The method proposed above provides a way for the value of the Old Testament to be realized in the lives of Christians.

By virtue of the above method a definition of biblical theology is suggested. Biblical theology is not a part of historical interpretation, although it is definitely a part of the interpretative process. It is the application of the discoveries and insights revealed through historical interpretation. Biblical theology is based upon and dependent upon historical interpretation. It is that part of the interpretative process which brings to bear upon the lives of concerned people the meaning of the Scripture.[1]

In addition, the general area of theology is touched by the process of interpretation suggested above. If the holistic view of the relationship between God and man suggested above[2] is an adequate center about which all else in the biblical materials and in theology revolve, then other areas of theology can be related to it. For example, the secular-sacred discussion which is going on in theological circles and which affects laymen more than they may realize will have an adequate perspective. Since the basis of theolgy is, in this view, the relationship between God and man and the expression of that relationship in relations between men, neither the secular side of life nor the spiritual side of life can be dominant. The secular is the very arena in which the spiritual finds expression. The spiritual is not to be relegated to some mystical union between God and man that only a few Christians are priviledged to have or that can be discovered only through so-called spiritual disciplines. The spiritual is that understanding of God which is expressed in the secular. It is not secular versus spiritual or even secular-spiritual. A better representation would be to overlay one upon the other in such a fashion that they cannot be separated.

Although the method presented above has been aimed primarily at the Old Testament, it can actually be used for the whole Bible, particularly if the major assumption of the method[3] is accepted. The interpretation of the New Testament suffers from problems of antiquity which are similar to those in the Old Testament and even the New Testament (at least, much of it) cannot be applied directly to the twentieth century.

The method presented above begins, first of all, with an influencing framework or viewpoint about the Bible. It is a way of looking at the Bible. Accordingly, one would regard the Bible as valuable for principles but not for direct application to specific problems today. For instance, one should not look for specific church organization in the New Testament and attempt to apply that organization directly to church life in the twentieth century. Rather, an attempt should be made to discover <u>principles</u> of a church organization in the Bible and then apply these principles to church structure in the twentieth century. This would coincide with the pluralism of church organization today. Many churches and many denominations with differing church structures and church organizations exist today and many of them are Christian. If this is so, then a logical conclusion is that there is no one right way of church structure or a biblical as opposed to a non-biblical way of organizing a church. However, the principles underlying the structure ought to be biblical. For instance, many biblical statements reveal that Christianity is a person-centered religion. The author of Psalm 8 realized that man, who is insignificant in the universe, is significant to God. Jesus' statement that the sabbath was made for man seems especially significant.[4] However, a concern for individuals can be expressed in different ways organizationally.

As one seeks principles in the Bible the answers to specific questions about behavior, which obviously involve the culture in which the person lives, may not be found. For instance, transplants of human organs from one person to another may raise serious moral and religious questions. Certainly the answers to these specific questions will not be found in the Bible. Rather, principles of behavior can be found which can be applied to specific situations and help guide one in finding answers to specific questions.

Not only is the method a way of looking at the Bible, the method focuses upon the Bible per se. In this method, the Bible itself must be read and studied. Thus, it will make for a greater appreciation of the Bible and will tend toward more accurate knowledge of the Bible. Although many Christians claim to be guided by the Bible, in fact, they often read into the Bible practices and ideas which come from outside the Bible.

As attention is focused upon the Bible with a viewpoint that grasps the whole Bible, there will be much less fragmentation of the Bible than there has been in the past both by specialists and laymen. Biblical scholarship has often been accused of fragmenting the Bible and to some extent this is true. However, in scholarship there is at present an emphasis on seeing books in their entirety as well as in their smaller units.[5]

Not only does this method focus attention on the Bible, but it makes virtually all the Bible available for significant use by Christians. Thus, it could bring the Old Testament into general use by laymen.[6] In practice, certain portions of the Bible are seldom used. For instance, the Song of Solomon and the laws in the Old Testament are not often used. But these passages, however obscure and unesthetic they may seem, can yield principles of behaviour and relationship to God which are meaningful and helpful to Christians. The Song of Solomon, for instance, elevates the idea of love and sexual relationships which makes it clear that every aspect of human love is honorable within the concept of marriage.[7] Perhaps a careful study and appreciation of the book might lead to a healthier attitude toward the place of sex in human relationships. The laws show how Israel attempted to interpret the idea of a holy God who demanded holy living. But the laws of Judaism also show that the behavior demanded by a holy God cannot be reduced simply to a code of laws. The principle here is not so much the specific laws of Israel as the intent. Their intent was to help Israelites live lives that would be honorable to a holy God.[8]

Not only is attention focused upon the Bible, the method discussed above provides a way

to interpret particular divisions of the Bible and
to deal with the problems peculiar to the divisions.
In prophecy, for instance, the concept of prediction
often overrules any other consideration, especially
among laymen. Prediction, which tends so easily
toward an uncontrolled allegorism, will be much less
necessary as a method of finding relevancy in the
prophets when one uses the method proposed above.
For instance, in such passages as Isaiah 53, Isaiah
7, and Isaiah 9, historical interpretation can be
given its fullest possible use. At the same time,
the concept of application makes readily accessible
a consideration of the importance of Jesus in the
understanding of these passages without minimizing
the original historical circumstances. The scholar
can use all his tools as intensively and extensively
as possible in understanding what these passages
meant in their own day. Then, by means of theological interpretation, the passages can be applied
to Jesus. Isaiah 53 speaks of a suffering servant,
one who would suffer vicariously for his people.
Whether the servant was an individual or the nation
and whether Jesus was immediately in view in the
original intention of these words, the concept of
servant can be applied to Jesus. One principle
that can be derived from this passage of scripture
is that God will redeem his people through the
ministry of a vicariously suffering servant. Application can be made to Jesus most uniquely, for
he was indeeed a vicariously suffering servant
through whom God intended to redeem people. However, principles derived through historical interpretation may make possible other applications also.
In Isaiah 53 the servant suffers for his own people.
Thus, the passage is applicable to any situation
in which God's people need to be redeemed. A
church, for instance, which has strayed from God's
will is, in a sense, in need of redemption. A
vicariously suffering servant may well be needed
to lead the church back to God. The experience of
some pastors in relationship to the racial problem
of the 1960's is an excellent example. A pastor
who wishes to apply the concept of God's love to
every man may well have to suffer for his people.
The concept of application after historical inter-

pretation is done frees the interpreter from the
need to resort to the concept of prediction or
other allegoristic interpretations in order to find
relevance in the prophets or any other passage of
scripture. Historical interpretation is not the
bane of relevance but the avenue through which relevance is found.

The method of reducing the Scripture to
principles will help protect the interpreter from
wanting duplicated in his own life the miraculous
(supernatural) occurrences recorded in Scripture.
The emphasis will be upon the religious experience
revealed by the supernatural occurrence rather than
upon the supernatural occurrence itself. As with
Elijah on Mount Carmel,[9] one can expect God to
vindicate faith without necessarily expecting it
in just the way the Bible describes Elijah's experience. The supernatural occurrence is not ruled
out by this method but it does tend to make the
interpreter look for the acitvity of God in natural
occurrences also.

As has already been suggested, relevance
must be involved in the work of each of three
groups: specialists, professionals, and laymen.
Biblical study by each group must be aimed at application of the Old Testament to present-day,
historical circumstances. Although scholars may
be somewhat unwilling to leave their scholarly pursuits to popularize their findings or to attempt
the application of their findings, if their findings are to be made available for use by professionals and laymen, they must keep in mind that
application is the end product of the interpretative process. Thus the work of the scholar is
not done until he has elicited from the Scripture
and stated some principles concerning the relationship between God and man.[10] On the other hand,
laymen must keep in mind that historical interpretation is the beginning of the interpretative
process. The application which the layman wants
to make is not properly begun until he has given
some consideration to the findings of historical
interpretation.

The professional is the man in the middle. He knows that he must come up with something applicable in every-day Christian life. His immediate task causes him to focus upon application. The time, effort, and cost of his academic training, however, gives him an inclination toward historical interpretation. But he may feel that the scholarly work is without relevance because the final step in historical interpretation has not been done. In too many cases principles which one could go to to find relevance have not been stated. Thus, the professional may turn away from the Bible and produce sermons which have a very tenuous connection to Scripture, or at least to the scripture chosen for a text. However, the professional who would seriously engage in biblical study beginning with historical interpretation can lay up a vast reservoir for sermon material and application to everyday Christian living.

The solution proposed above makes possible a drawing together of laymen, professionals, and scholars. The solutuion proposed here does this by introducing the laymen to at least the basics of historical biblical research. Thus, the work of the scholar does not forever remain a mystery to him. Further, it makes provision in one process for an adequate appreciation by the scholar of the so-called spiritual element (concerning which most laymen are interested) of the Bible without denigrating historical research. By seeing interpretation as a process beginning with historical interpretation and ending in application, each of the three groups can more readily appreciate the work of the other. Each can see in this process the necessity of all the parts of the process.

For the professional, the traditional task of sermon preparation may be clarified if not made easier. If historical and theological interpretation are taken together as two parts of a whole, then preparation for preaching must include both parts. If the historical task is incomplete or not done at all, eisegesis may very well be the end result with the preacher saying things that the

Bible does not say.

The methodology, which is useful to laymen, can be just as useful to professionals whether they are trained in the technical study of the Old Testament or not. They will be able to do biblical preaching more easily for at least two reasons. Biblical preaching will be clarified,[11] and the method will allow the professional to use the knowledge he has although it may not be as technical or as developed as that of the specialist. The professional may very well be encouraged to do historical interpretation because he will know that it leads to the very thing he wants--application of the Bible to the lives of those who hear him from week to week. Further, the applications of the Old Testament which he makes may be more adequate because they are based upon historical interpretation.

Further, the structure of the sermon may also be affected. A sermon may legitimately be an exegesis of a text with its resultant application or may present only the application. Probably the sermon should seldom be historical interpretation alone. However, the teaching ministry of the Church can and should present historical interpretation of the Bible.

The Old Testament is relevant to the Christian faith. The possibilities open to Christianity when the process of interpretation is understood and practiced are enormous.

[1] Cf. Stendahl, "Biblical Theology," who places biblical theology within historical interpretation and seems more intent on differentiating it from systematic theology than in saying how the Bible may be made relevant to the twentieth century. He seems to give to systematic theology the task of determining relevance.

[2] See above, pp. 143-145.

[3] See above, pp. 114-118. The assumption is that the Testaments are united because they both express the same religion.

[4] Mark 2:27; Matt. 12:1-8.

[5] Cf. Brownlee, *The Meaning of the Qumran Scrolls for the Bible*, p. 256. Brownlee's major emphasis, which he derives from an emphasis he believes is revealed by the Qumran scroll of Isaiah, is upon all sixty-six chapters of Isaiah rather than the smaller literary units.

[6] This does not mean that all parts will yield their relevance with equal facility.

[7] Cf. such usually disparate viewpoints as that of Edward J. Young, *An Introduction to the Old Testament* (Grand Rapids: Wm. B. Eerdmans Publishing Co., 1956), p. 327, and Bentzen, *Introduction to the Old Testament*, II, 182. Young states, "The Song does celebrate the dignity and purity of human love." Bentzen affirms, "It is in reality narrow-minded to advance the question of the 'theological significance of the poems'. Why not thank God, because he among the sacred books has also given us words of love?" Anderson, *Understanding the Old Testament*, pp. 494-95, has a similar viewpoint.

[8] Cf. Anderson, *Understanding the Old Testament*, p. 61, "The Law . . . was the form that was used for expressing the covenant bond."

[9] Cf. Smart, *Dialogue*, p. 87.

[10] Kaiser, "Old Testament Exegesis," p. 32.

[11] Cf. Toombs, <u>The Old Testament in Christian Preaching</u>, p. 15, <u>whose definition is nearly the same as that suggested here</u>. H. C. Brown, Jr., <u>A Quest for Reformation in Preaching</u>, p. 71, defines a direct biblical sermon similarly. "Only by moving correctly from the grammatical-historical 'then' to the relevant 'now' can a sermon be a direct Biblical sermon." However, Brown seems to emphasize direct application of Scripture. Cf. above, pp. 145-147.

SELECTED BIBLIOGRAPHY

## History of Interpretation

### Books

Barth, Markus. Conversation with the Bible, New York: Holt, Rinehart, and Winston, 1964.

Blackman, E. C. Marcion and His influence. London: S.P.C.K., 1948.

Bonsirven, Joseph. Exegese Rabbininque et Exegese Paulinienne. Paris: Beauchesne et ses fils, 1939.

Cheyne, T.K. Founders of Old Testament Criticism. New York: Charles Scribner's Sons, 1893.

Danielou, Jean. Origen. Translated by Walter Mitchell. New York: Sheed and Ward, 1955.

Dodd, C. H. According to the Scriptures: The Substructure of New Testament Theology. London: Nisbet & Co., Ltd., 1952.

Duff, Archibald. History of Old Testament Criticism. London: Watts and Company, 1910.

Ellis, E. Earle. Paul's Use of the Old Testament. Grand Rapids: Wm. B. Eerdmans Publishing Company, 1957.

Farrar, Frederick W. History of Interpretation. Reprint from 1886 edition published by E. P. Dutton, New York. Grand Rapids: Baker Book House, 1961.

Gilbert, George Holley. Interpretation of the Bible. New York: n.p., 1908.

Grant, R. M. *The Bible in the Church*. New York: The Macmillan Company, 1948.

Grant, W. M. *The Bible of Jesus*. New York: George H. Doran Company, 1927.

Gray, Edward M. *Old Testament Criticism*. New York: Harpers, 1923.

Harnack, A. von. *Marcion: Das Evangelium vom fremden Gott*. Leipzig: J. C. Hinrichs, 1921 and 1924.

Kerr, Hugh T. *The first Systematic Theologian: Origen of Alexandria*. Princeton, N. J.: Princeton Theological Seminary, 1958.

Knox, John. *Marcion and the New Testament*. Chicago: The University of Chicago Press, 1942.

Kooinan, Willem Jan. *Luther and the Bible*. Translated by John Schmidt. Philadelphia: Muhlenberg Press, 1961.

Kraus, Hans-Joichim. *Gestchiechte der Historisch-kritischen Erforschung des Alten Testaments von der Reformation bis zur Gegenwart*. Neukirchen Kreis Moers: Buchhandlung des Erziehungsvereins, 1956.

Lindars, Barnabas. *New Testament Apologetic*. Philadelphia: Westminster Press, 1961.

Smalley, Beryl. *The Study of the Bible in the Middle Ages*. 2nd ed. Oxford: Basil Blackwell, 1952.

Smith, Henry Preserved. *Essays in Biblical Interpretation*. Boxton: Marshall Jones Company, 1921.

Spicq, P. C. *Esquisse d'une Histoire de L'Exegese Latine au Moyen Age*. Bibliotheque Thomiste, XXVI. Paris: Librairie Philosophique J. Vrin, 1944.

Stendahl, Krister. The School of St. Matthew. Lund: C. W. K. Gleerup, 1954.

Terry, Milton S. Biblical Hermeneutics. Grand Rapids: Zondervan Publishing House, n.d.

Wenham, J. W. The Lord's View of the Old Testament. London: Tyndale Press, 1955.

Wilson, R. S. Marcion. London: Clarke, 1933.

Wolfson, Harry Austryn. Philo, Foundations of Religious Philosophy in Judaism, Christianity, and Islam. Rev. ed. Cambridge, Mass.: Harvard University Press, 1948.

Wood, James D. The Interpretation of the Bible. London: Gerald Duckworth and Co., Ltd., 1958.

## Articles

Barth, Markus. "The Old Testament in Hebrews." Current Issues in New Testament Interpretation. Edited by William Klassen and Graydon F. Snyder. New York: Harper & Row, Publishers, 1962.

De Bries, S. J. "Biblical Criticism, History of." The Interpreter's Dictionary of the Bible. Vol. I.

Geffcken, Johannes. "Allegory." Encyclopedia of Religion and Ethics. Vol. I.

Grant, R. M. "The Place of the Old Testament in Early Christianity." Interpretation, V (April, 1951), 194.97.

Grobel, K. "Biblical Criticism." The Interpreter's Dictionary of the Bible. Vol. I.

_____. "Interpretation." The Interpreter's Dictionary of the Bible. Bol. I.

Jewett, Paul K. "Concerning the Allegorical Interpretation of Scripture." *Westminster Theological Journal*, XVII (November, 1954), 1-21.

"Marcion and the Marcionite Churches." *Encyclopaedia Brittanica*. 1959. Vol. XIV.

Smart, James D. "The Death and Rebirth of Old Testament Theology.: *Journal of Religion*, XXIII, No. 1 (1943), 1-11; XXXIII, No. 2 (1943), 125.36.

Smith, Morton. "The Present State of Old Testament Studies." *Journal of Biblical Literature*, LXXXVIII (March, 1969), 19-35.

## Tools of Interpretation

Danker, Frederick W. *Multipurpose Tools for Bible Study*. St. Louis: Concordia Publishing House, 1966.

Kelly, Balmer H., and Miller, Donald G. *Tools for Bible Study*. Richmond, Va.: John Knox Press, 1956.

## Methodology of Interpretation

### Books

Achtemeier, Paul, and Achtemeier, Elizabeth. *The Old Testament Books of Our Faith*. New York: Abingdon Press, 1962.

Anderson, Bernhard W., ed. *The Old Testament and Christian Faith*. New York: Harper and Row, 1963.

Barr, James. *Old and New in Interpretation, a Study of the Two Testaments*. London: SCM Press, Ltd., 1966.

Braaten, Carl E. History and Hermeneutics. Vol. II of New Directions in Theology. Edited by William Hordern. 6 vols. Philadelphia: Westminster Press, 1966.

Bright, John. The Authority of the Old Testament. Nashville: Abingdon Press, 1967.

_____. Early Israel in Recent History Writing. Studies in Biblical Theology No. 19, London: SCM Press, Ltd., 1956.

Brown, Raymond E. The Sensus Plenior of Sacred Scripture. Baltimore, Md.: St. Mary's University, 1955.

Brownlee, William Hugh. The Meaning of the Qumran Scrolls for the Bible. New York: Oxford University Press, 1964.

Dodd, C. H. The Bible To-Day. Cambridge: University Press, 1946.

Fisher, Fred. How to Interpret the New Testament. Philadelphia: Westminster Press, 1967.

Guthrie, Harvey H., Jr. Israel's Sacred Songs. New York: The Seabury Press, 1966.

Hahn, Herbert F. The Old Testament in Modern Research. Expanded ed. Philadelphia: Fortress Press, 1966.

Hanson, R. P. C. Allegory and Event. London: SCM Press, Ltd., 1959.

Herbert, A. G. The Authority of the Old Testament. London: Faber and Faber, Ltd., 1947.

Lampe, G. W. H., and Woollcombe, K. J. Essays on on Typology. Studies in Biblical Theology No. 22. Naperville, Ill.: Alec. R. Allenson, Inc., 1957.

Lys, Daniel. The Meaning of the Old Testament. Nashville: Abingdon Press, 1967.

Mickelsen, A. Berkley. *Interpreting the Bible*. Philadelphia: Westminster Press, 1963.

Phillips, Godfrey E. *The Old Testament in the World Church*. London: Lutterworth Press, 1942.

Ramm, Bernard. *Protestant Biblical Interpretation*. Rev. ed. Boston: W. A. Wilde Company, 1956.

Richardson, Alan. *The Bible in the Age of Science*. Philadelphia: Westminster Press, 1961.

Robinson, H. Wheeler. *Inspiration and Revelation in the Old Testament*. Oxford: Clarendon Press, 1946.

Rowley, H. H. *The Unity of the Bible*. London: Carey Kingsgate Press, Ltd., 1953.

Smart, James D. *The Old Testament in Dialogue with Modern Man*. Philadelphia: Westminster Press, 1964.

_____. *The Interpretation of Scripture*. Philadelphia: Westminster Press, 1961.

Tasker, R. V. G. *The Old Testament in the New Testament*. Rev. ed. London: SCM Press, Ltd., 1954.

Toombs, Lawrence E. *The Old Testament in Christian Preaching*. Philadelphia: Westminster Press, 1961.

Westermann, Claus, ed. *Essays on Old Testament Hemeneutics*. Richmond: John Knox Press, 1963.

Wright, G. Ernest. *God Who Acts*. Studies in Biblical Theology No. 8. London: SCM Press, Ltd., 1952.

## Articles

Barr, James. "Revelation Through History in the Old Testament and in Modern Theolgy." Interpretation, XVII (April, 1963), 193-205.

Bright, John. "An Exercise in Hermeneutics." Interpretation, XX (April, 1966), 188-210.

Burrows, Millar. "The Task of Biblical Theolgy." Journal of Bible and Religion, XIV (February, 1946), 13-15.

Bultmann, Rudolf. "Is Exegesis without Presuppositions Possible?" Existence and Faith. Translated by Schubert M. Ogden. New York: Meridian Books, Inc., 1960.

_____. "The Problem of Hermeneutics." Essays: Philosophical and Theological. Translated by James C. G. Greig. London: SCM Press, Ltd., 1955.

_____. "Prohecy and Fulfillment.: Essays on Old Testament Hermeneutics. Edited by Claus Westermann. Richmond, Va.: John Knox Press, 1963.

_____. "The Significance of the Old Testament for the Christian Faith." The Old Testament and Christian Faith. Edited by Bernhard W. Anderson. New York: Harper and Row, 1963.

Cadbury, Henry J. "The Peril of Archaizing Ourselves." Interpretation, III (July, 1949), 331-37.

Craig, Clarence T. "Biblical Theology and the Rise of Histoicism." Journal of Biblical Literature, LXII (December, 1943), 281-94.

Darbyshire, J. R. "Typology." Encyclopedia of Religion and Ethics. 1922. Vol. XII.

Dentan, Robert C. "Typolgy--Its Use and Abuse." Anglican Theological Review, XXXIV (October, 1952), 211-17.

Fairweather, Eugene R. "Christianity and the Supernatural." New Theology No. 1. Edited by Martin E. Marty and Dean G. Peerman. New York: The Macmillan Company, 1964.

Filson, Floyd V. "Unity of the Old and the New Testaments." Interpretation, V (April, 1951), 138-52.

Freedman, David Noel. "The Interpretation of Scripture: On Method in Biblical Studies: The Old Testament." Interpretation, XVII (July, 1963), 309-18.

Haller, Eduard. "On the Interpretative Task." Interpretation, XXI (April, 1967), 158-66.

Hummel, Horace D. "Survey of Recent Literature." The Old Testament in Modern Research. Expanded ed. Herbert F. Hahn. Philadelphia: Fortress Press, 1966.

Jepsen, Alfred. "The Scientific Study of the Old Testament." Essays on Old Testament Hermeneutics. Edited by Claus Westermann. Richmond, Va.: John Knox Press, 1963.

Kaiser, Otto. "Old Testament Exegesis.: Exegetical Method. Translated by E. V. H. Goetchius. New York: The Seabury Press, 1967.

Kelsey, David H. Review of The Authority of the Old Testament, by John Bright, Journal of Biblical Literature, LXXXVI (June, 1967), 217-18.

McCasland, S. Vernon. "The Unity of the Scriptures." *Journal of Biblical Literature*, LXXIII (March, 1954), 1-10.

Markus, R. A. "Presuppositions of the Typological Approach to Scripture." *Church Quarterly Review*, CLVIII (October-December, 1957), 442-51.

Marsh, John. "History and Interpretation." *Biblical Authority for Today*. Edited by Alan Richardson and W. Schweitzer. London: SCM Press, Ltd., 1951.

Michalson, Carl. "Bultmann against Marcion." *The Old Testament and Christian Faith*. Edited by Bernhard W. Anderson. New York: Harper and Row, 1963.

Miller, Donald G. "How to Study the Bible." *Introduction to the Bible*. Vol. I of *The Layman's Bible Commentary*. Edited by Balmer H. Kelly. 25 vols. Richmond, Va.: John Knox Press, 1959.

Muilenburg, James. "Preface to Hermeneutics." *Journal of Biblical Literautre*, LXXVII (March, 1958), 18-26.

Rad, Gerhard von. "Typological Interpretation of the Old Testament." *Essays on Old Testament Hermeneutics*. Edited by Claus Westermann. Richmond, Va.: John Knox Press, 1963.

Ramm, Bernard L. "Biblical Interpretation." *Baker's Dictionary of Practical Theology*. Edited by Ralph G. Turnbull. Grand Rapids: Baker Book House, 1967.

Reumann, John. "Introduction." *Biblical Problems and Biblical Preaching*. C. K. Barrett. Biblical Series No. 6, reprint of Foundery Pamphlet No. 7. Philadelphia: Fortress Press, 1964.

Rylaarsdam, J. Coert. "Preface to Hermeneutics." Journal of Religion, XXX (April, 1950), 79-89.

_____. "The Problem of Faith and History in Biblical Interpretation." Journal of Biblical Literature, LXXVII (March, 1958), 26-32.

Smart, James D. "The Need for a Biblical Theology." Religion in Life, XXVI (Winter, 1956-57), 22-30.

Stendahl, Krister. "Biblical Theology, Contemporary." The Interpreter's Dictionary of the Bible. Vol. I.

_____. "Implications of Form-Criticism and Tradition-Criticism for Biblical Interpretation." Journal of Biblical Literature, LXXVII (March, 1958), 33-38.

_____. "Method in the Study of Biblical Theology." The Bible in Modern Scholarship. Edited by J. Philip Hyatt. Nashville: Abingdon Press, 1965.

Wilder, Amos N. "New Testament Hermeneutics Today." Current Issues in New Testament Interpretation. Edited by William Klassen and Graydon F. Snyder. New York: Harper & Row, 1962.

Wright, G. Ernest. "Archeology and Old Testament Studies." Journal of Biblical Literature, LXXVII (March, 1958), 39-51.

_____. "Modern Issues in Biblical Studies: History and the Patriarchs." Expository Times, LXXI (July, 1960), 292-96.

_____. "Old Testament Scholarship in Prospect." Journal of Bible and Religion, XXVIII (1960), 182-93.

Wright, G. Ernest. "The Problem of Archaizing Ourselves." *Interpretation*, III (October, 1949), 450-56.

Wolff, Hans Walter. "The Hermeneutics of the Old Testament." *Essays on Old Testament Hermeneutics*. Edited by Claus Westermann. Richmond, Va.: John Knox Press, 1963.

## INDEX

Alexandria, 38f, 52n61
Allegorical interpretation, 28, 30f, 34, 36, 37-42, 60n161, 73, 76, 78, 95, 128, 181f
Antioch, School of, 30f, 39, 43, 52n61
Application, 11, 17n34, 36, 42f, 81, 96, 101, 112-114, 120f, 129f, 132-134, 138, 142-158, 178, 181-184
Archaism, 67-68, 99n30
Authority of the Bible, 2, 127, 156, 177

Barr, James, 68, 70
Barth, Karl, 5, 8, 9, 24, 128
Biblical theology, 11, 17n34, 20, 70f, 73, 111f, 128, 177f, 185n1
Bright, John, 114, 116, 122, 127-131
Bultmann, Rudolf, 87-95, 139

Canon, 121f
Christological interpretation, 33, 35, 37, 72, 125, 128
Context, 132, 135f, 158
Critical interpretation, 63, see also historical interpretation, literal interpretation, historical grammatical interpretation, modern critical interpretation

Demythologizing, 37, 94
Dentan, Robert, 67
Dialogical interpretation, 24, 27
Dodd, C. H., 22

Eisegesis, 138
Ellis, E. Earle, 23
Exegesis, 17n36, 25f, 36f, 42, 111-114, 128-130, 132-139, 141f, 147, 149-151, 154f, 184
Existentialism, 27, 72, 87-95, 139

Faith, 3, 35f
Faith and history, 3
Faith and reason, 9, 156, 177

Hermeneutics, definition, 10f, 17n34
Historical critical interpretation, 4f, 9, 11
Historical grammatical interpretation, 24, 35
Historical interpretation, 17n34, 21, 24, 27, 30f, 34, 36, 42-44, 73, 76, 80, 95f, 111-114, 123f, 126, 128-132, 134f, 137, 142, 156, 177, 181-184, see also exegesis, critical interpretation
Hittite suzerainty treaties, 144

Inspiration, 30, 86, 119
Interpretation, circular, 137-139, 143

Jewish interpretation, 28, 30-32, 34, 36

Literal interpretation, 28, 30-32, 34, 36, 41-43, 60n161, 84, 86
Luther, Martin, 33-36, 43

Marcion, 4, 27-30, 36, 43, 91, 94f, 116, 127, 128
Modern critical interpretation 63-70, see also critical interpretation, modern scientific interpretation
Modern scientific interpretation, 17n34, 33

Origen, 39-41, 75
Outlining, 140f, 151f, 158

Pedagogical use of the Old Testament, 84, 89-91, 130
Pesher method of interpretation, 23, 26
Presuppositions, 92f, 138f, 149-151, 153, 156, see also subjectivism
Principles, 111, 121-123, 132f, 138, 142f, 145, 147-150, 154-157, 179, 182
Promise and fulfillment, 73, 77, 87-89, 115

Ramm, Bernard, 33, 119
Rationalism, 75
Reinterpretation, 21
Religious experience, 141-145, 147f, 150, 152, 154, 156, 158, 180, 182
Re-presentation, 74f

3728

Revelation, 117f, 120-122
Revelation, progressive, 87
Revelation through history, 68-70

Sensus plenior, 72, 81-87, 128
Smart, James, 2, 14n14, 69f, 78, 99n27, 100n37, 113, 119, 125-127, 131
Spiritual interpretation, 31
Stendahl, Krister, 10, 22, 121
Subjectivism, 31, 76, 86, 93, 95, 118-120, 128, 156, see also presuppositions

Theological interpretation, 5, 9-11, 17n34, 27, 37, 43f, 63-65, 70-74, 80f, 95f, 111-114, 123f, 126, 128f, 131f, 134, 142, 156, 181, 183, see also application, biblical theology, Christological interpretation
Tools for Bible study, 157f
Typological interpretation, 31, 57n133, 67, 71-83, 128, 132

Unity of the Testaments, 34f, 48n17, 67, 72, 75, 82, 114-118, 125, 130f, 142, 144, 157, 174n161, 185

Victorines, 31-33, 39, 43
Vriezen, Th. C., 24

Wellhausen, Julius, 8, 66, 112
Wright, G. E., 68, 78f, 100n37